JOURNAL FOR THE STUDY OF THE OLD TESTAMENT SUPPLEMENT SERIES
202

Sheffield Academic Press

Law and Liminality in the Bible

Nanette Stahl

Journal for the Study of the Old Testament
Supplement Series 202

For my parents David and Hannah Stahl
in loving memory

Copyright © 1995 Sheffield Academic Press

Published by Sheffield Academic Press Ltd
Mansion House
19 Kingfield Road
Sheffield, S11 9AS
England

Printed on acid-free paper in Great Britain
by Bookcraft Ltd
Midsomer Norton, Bath

British Library Cataloguing in Publication Data

A catalogue record for this book is available
from the British Library

ISBN 1-85075-561-2

CONTENTS

ACKNOWLEDGMENTS

This book has benefited from the help and support of many people. My debt to Chana Kronfeld can scarcely be overstated. Her unfailing interest and ongoing involvement helped me see this project through to completion. I will always recall with fondness and pleasure the many hours we spent deep in discussion over the intricacies and nuances of the poetics of law in the Bible. The breadth of her scholarship is an inspiration. I am grateful to Robert Alter for his encouragement and support. His seminars in biblical literature at the University of California at Berkeley inspired me to undertake this study. Daniel Boyarin's insights and suggestions were most helpful and appreciated.

There are others to whom I am also indebted: Netta Dor-Shav, without whose support and encouragement I would never have undertaken this project; Howard Eilberg-Schwartz, Wolfgang Heimpel, David Biale, William W. Hallo, J.H. Chajes, F.W. Dobbs-Allsopp, Steven D. Fraade, Orin Gensler and Peter Solomon all shared their thoughts and vast knowledge. Any errors are of course my own. To the Taubman Fellowship of the University of California at Berkeley I am indebted for financial assistance. My nephews Jacob and Daniel gave much love, and provided much needed diversion, throughout this entire undertaking.

ABBREVIATIONS

AB	Anchor Bible
BDB	F. Brown, S.R. Driver and C.A. Briggs, *Hebrew and English Lexicon of the Old Testament*
HTR	*Harvard Theological Review*
HUCA	*Hebrew Union College Annual*
JBL	*Journal of Biblical Literature*
JJS	*Journal of Jewish Studies*
JNES	*Journal of Near Eastern Studies*
PLMA	*Proceedings of the Modern Language Association of America*
VT	*Vetus Testamentum*

Chapter 1

DIFFERENCE IN BIBLICAL DISCOURSE

The enactments of God are purposefully embedded; they stand in fruitful interaction with the narrative mass...and share their themes with it.

J.P. Fokkelman[1]

The Israelites placed their laws within a narrative context, in a book along with stories, genealogies, poems and prophecies, and even, in Exodus, within the same portion of the book. Are we good readers when we split up what has been put together this way? Is it not up to us to try to understand what that putting together might imply?

Gabriel Josipovici[2]

Law occupies a major part of the Pentateuch, yet on the whole very little attention has been paid to the role it plays as a genre in relation to other genres of biblical discourse, or in biblical poetics in general. Are the legal instructions purposefully embedded in the 'narrative mass'? Why are so many voices and genres 'put together'?[3] This unexplored interaction of law and narrative in the Bible, as well as the many voices of law itself, are the central concerns of this study.

In the passages quoted above, Fokkelman and Josipovici express an often overlooked intuition about the polyphonic

1. J.P. Fokkelman, 'Exodus', in R. Alter and F. Kermode (eds.), *The Literary Guide to the Bible* (Cambridge, MA: Harvard University Press, 1987), p. 62.

2. G. Josipovici, *The Book of God: A Response to the Bible* (New Haven, CT: Yale University Press, 1988), p. 92.

3. Fokkelman does note that 'what we need to do here is to examine the relation of speech, using the tools of current textual and narrative theory, and not to detach embedded speech from its textural setting, even if it comes from the character of God' (Fokkelman, 'Exodus', p. 62).

nature of the biblical text; in particular, that the communications between God and humanity are neither monolithic nor uniform. What does it mean for a monotheistic text to valorize discursive plural voices so strongly and consistently? I am convinced that the biblical mixture of genres and voices is the manifestation of a series of underlying tensions, a way to allow for the expression of a complex, even contradictory, ideology. Law, perhaps more than any other discursive practice in the Bible, plays a crucial role in articulating and highlighting these tensions.

The relation of law to other generic formations in the Bible reveals a profound ambivalence concerning the divine experiment with creation in general and with human creation in particular. The view that emerges is at the same time optimistic and celebratory yet deeply pessimistic and disillusioned. As presented in biblical narrative, every attempt on the part of the deity to establish a relationship with humanity—or to initiate change after some failure—is fraught with the tension between promise and jeopardy.

In the Bible, auspicious beginnings always seem to fade into disappointing endings. Nevertheless, from the perspective of biblical theology, divine attempts to forge a connection with the human cannot cease. I will refer to these times of new beginnings and transition, these critical phases in the divine–human relationship, as liminal moments. The insertion of law into narrative discourse appears to be most common—and most significant—at precisely such junctures in the Pentateuch, and accordingly these particular liminal moments will be the focus of my study.

Liminal moments are of pivotal importance precisely because of their dynamic, inter-categorical position as transitions leading from one period to another.[4] Such moments may be brief and enigmatic, as when Moses and his family, returning to Egypt from Midian, encounter a menacing supernatural being—actually referred to in the Bible as God himself (Exod. 4.24-26); or they

4.   See H.-U. Gumbrecht and U. Link-Heer (eds.), *Epochenschwellen und Epochenstrukturen im Diskurs der Literatur- und Sprachhistorie* (Frankfurt am Main: Suhrkamp, 1985); and P. Orecchioni, 'Dates-clés et glissements chronologiques', in J. Dubois *et al.* (eds.), *Analyse de la périodisation littéraire* (Paris: Éditions Universitaires, 1972).

may be detailed and elaborate, as in the account of the post-diluvian covenant with Noah (Gen. 9.1-17). The depiction of a liminal moment may even consist of more than one narrative, as with the two versions of creation (Gen. 1.1–2.4; 2.4–3.24). All liminal moments, however, share some defining characteristics: they are concerned with transition, and function as focal points of the biblical vision of the often tenuous, always dynamic relationship between God and his elect.

Essentially, these moments involve an attempt at divine–human communication and interaction. They are far from being uniformly positive, however; rather, they are fraught with ambiguities and the threat of instability. This could be expected within a system-theoretical view of change,[5] where transitions enable continuity even as they destabilize the system. So these moments stand out as much for the risks they involve as for their promise of progress. For example, the episode of Jacob's struggle with the angel, which transforms Jacob into Israel, the eponymous father, is characterized by conflict and potentially mortal danger to Jacob: though he emerges victorious, he is permanently maimed (Gen. 32.33). His victory is part and parcel of his injury, and each is colored by the other. As I will demonstrate in Chapter 5, promise and jeopardy are juxtaposed in this episode, and the resulting instability is characteristic of all such moments in the Bible. Typically, narratives depicting points of transition in biblical history are profoundly ambivalent: even as they presage a new chapter, these narratives echo contrapuntal themes that put the success of the undertaking in doubt from the very start. The biblical liminal moment does not deliver a unitary message; it is the unharmonized sum of its conflicting parts.

It is no coincidence that law appears as a component of liminal moments in the Pentateuch. Indeed, legal material appears with such regularity at crucial turning points that its absence takes on significance. A good case in point is the tower of Babel (Gen. 11.1-9). This episode, like other liminal moments, marks the end of one period in biblical history and the beginning of another, has serious implications for the divine–human relationship, and contains distinct mythopoeic elements. But

5.   See Gumbrecht and Link-Heer (eds.), *Epochenschwellen*.

there are crucial differences: in other such episodes God or his agent interacts directly with humans; God never interacts in any way with the tower builders of Babel. He acts upon them—by dispersing them—but never speaks to them, a crucial omission given the fundamentally communicative nature of biblical law. Indeed, it would seem from the text that they never understand what happens to them or why. The tower builders are ultimately denied communication with God and with each other. Given God's utter withdrawal from this civilization, law—the ultimate form of divine communication—has no role to play. This absence thus dramatizes the linguistic nihilism which is at the core of the story, just as the presence of legal discourse at other liminal moments in biblical narrative history generically signals the continuation of a tension-ridden, but ultimately enduring dialogue.

Law is thus one of the distinctive features of foundational biblical narratives. And an examination of the poetics of the legal inserts—of their precise location in such narratives, and their interaction not only with the particular passage in which they are embedded, but with other foundational narratives as well—indicates that they fulfill a complex role. These legal pronouncements serve not just as a source of stability and order in an imperfect, chaotic world. Biblical liminal moments are inherently flawed; the associated legal inserts reflect and resonate with the ambiguity of the narratives themselves. For example, the laws given to Noah after the flood, which include the prohibition against murder (Gen. 9.1-17), inaugurate a new era in human history; yet they are presented in a way that holds out little hope that the future will be much different from the past. Rather these laws are articulated against a narrative background that acknowledges that 'the devisings of man's mind are evil from his youth' (8.21) and are highly pessimistic about the possibility of changing this human propensity. The laws echo the destabilizing themes implicit in the narrative and work to further undermine the message of healing and renewal at the very moment it is articulated.

This undercutting quality of the legal inserts can be discerned in both texture and structure. Texturally, the rhetoric of the legal statement calls into question the seemingly optimistic overt theme of the foundational narrative. In many cases, though not all, the legal insert itself includes both an affirming and a negating statement. For example, the mandate to Noah after the flood at first seems to allow unrestricted consumption of all that nature has to offer—'Every creature that lives shall be yours to eat...' (Gen. 9.3)—but this grant is immediately modified in the verse 'You must not, however, eat flesh with its life-blood in it' (אך־בשר בנפשו דמו לא תאכלו) (9.4). On the structural level, the Noahide law embodies the dynamics of permissiveness and restraint that appear in the relationship between the two primeval legal pronouncements of the creation stories. The injunction to Noah begins (9.1-3) with a repetition of the divine charge from Gen. 1.28: 'Be fertile and increase and fill the earth' (פרו ורבו ומלאו את־הארץ); but then (9.4) echoes the restraining theme of the prohibition in the account of Eden: 'Of every tree of the garden you are free to eat: but as for the tree of knowledge of good and bad, you must not eat of it...' (מכל עץ הגן אכל תאכל ומעץ הדעת טוב ורע לא תאכל) (2.16-17). The Noahide injunction even duplicates the syntax of the Eden prohibition, and the two are further linked by the theme of death which predominates in both. In short, the legal inserts in the post-diluvian narrative present a complex network of linkages that work to affirm and simultaneously to undermine the message of renewal which is the primary theme of these passages. In one form or another, this is characteristic of all liminal moments in the Pentateuch.

In addition to highlighting the tension inherent in moments of major transition, law also serves to temper the mythopoeic overtones of these narratives, in which God is such a dramatized, active character. Herbert N. Schneidau argues that 'the Law was manifestly an attempt to stabilize and sacralize the social ideology and thus substitute for myth...'[6] but I would argue that law in the Bible does not so much replace myth as neutralize it. Through law, the Bible undercuts (or perhaps more accurately cuts down to size) not only mythic materials borrowed from the surrounding cultures but also the mythopoeic potential of its own narratives. In passages

6. H.N. Schneidau, *Sacred Discontent: The Bible and Western Tradition* (Baton Rouge, LA: Louisiana State University Press, 1976), p. 14.

depicting God in highly anthropomorphic terms, legal material sets boundaries between the divine and the human, and so transforms mythmaking into historiography. Within the biblical worldview, human ability to establish a connection with the great constitutive moments of the past can no longer be solely through myth but also—and from the monotheistic point of view primarily—through law. In Israelite culture, it is not only history that legitimates law, but law that legitimates history.[7]

Law plays a defining role in all the liminal moments discussed in this study. In the two creation stories (Gen. 1-2.4a; 2.4b-24) law points up the two almost diametrically opposed biblical visions of the divine–human experiment. The legal component of the post-diluvian narrative (Gen. 9.1-7) elaborates on this dual vision while focusing primarily on the more pessimistic side. The interplay between law and narrative is perhaps most extensive in the account of the revelation at Sinai, which like the creation story, is divided into two parts (Exod. 19.1–20.23; 34). In each, law serves not only to celebrate the institution of a covenant between God and Israel, but also to voice reservations concerning Israel's capacity to remain faithful to that covenant. Finally, in the account of Jacob's struggle with the angel (Gen. 32.25-33), alone of all the liminal moments I discuss, law appears as third-person narrative rather than direct embedded speech. Nevertheless, the legal component of this most mysterious and intriguing moment fills a role similar to that of law in other such moments: it celebrates Jacob's 'victory' while at the same time voicing ambivalence concerning the relationship inaugurated as a result of the struggle.

Why does law play such a crucial role within the ambivalent biblical worldview? As the textual enactment of God's communications, law is both the agent of divine order and the locus of an underlying theological tension. Through law, God

---

7.   D. Damrosch examines the transformation of epic into historical narrative in his book *The Narrative Covenant: Transformations of Genre in the Growth of Biblical Literature* (Ithaca, NY: Cornell University Press, 1987), but his focus is on ancient Near Eastern pagan cultures. Damrosch's chapter on 'Law and Narrative in the Priestly Work' does examine the subtle intermingling of law and historical narrative in the Priestly strand, but fails to address the demythologizing aspect of the biblical legal material.

attempts yet again to set the world right. Yet the very wording and structure of the law, and the interactions of legal units with the narrative frame, reveal that law is also an agent of disruption and destabilization.

The most common construction of the generic tension between law and narrative in the Bible is that the law is undermined by the narrative that enacts it. The paradigmatic example is the frequent reversal of the laws of primogeniture (as laid down in Deut. 21.15-17), a theme that runs through the narratives of the entire biblical corpus (for example, the preference of Abel over Cain, Isaac over Ishmael, Jacob over Esau, etc.).[8] This reversal so embodies the nomos, the normative discursive practice of biblical narrative, that one might even say it becomes a necessary condition for a protagonist who would transform himself into a hero and achieve his divinely ordained mission. This is well recognized. What has not been noted hitherto, however, is that this dialogism between law and narrative can be, and often is, bilateral: not only can narrative undercut law, but law can also reverse the ideological and ethical import of biblical narrative. Furthermore, the legal texts within themselves are fraught with the same sort of tension that exists between law and narrative. It is as if biblical law encapsulated the dissonance of the competing voices of the culture that enunciated it.

If biblical law, the very enactment of God's will, can itself be a moment of disruption of authority, surely this has some bearing on the literary and theological norms of the canon. This tension between the stabilizing and destabilizing potential of law is deeply rooted in the overall theological struggle in the Bible as a whole. Conflicting or divergent voices do not just appear somehow in the text, subversively; rather they are an inherent part of the biblical system. This thesis expands, in a sense, on Ilana Pardes's conception of biblical voices as a 'tense dialogue between the dominant patriarchal discourses of the Bible and

8.   David Biale and Robert Cover discuss this puzzling phenomenon of ongoing friction between law and narrative in the biblical text. See D. Biale, *Eros and the Jews: From Biblical Israel to Contemporary America* (New York: Basic Books, 1992), chapter 1; and R.M. Cover, 'Nomos and Narrative', *Harvard Law Review* 97.4 (1983), pp. 19-25.

counter female voices which attempt to offer other truths'.[9] It also elaborates on the work of Mieke Bal who argues, 'What went wrong in the history of the reception [of biblical texts] is precisely the repression of...the heterogeneous ideology of the text, which had to be turned into a monolithic one'.[10] But I want to extend the recovery of biblical heterogeneity beyond the matter of narrative genres and marginalized female voices to other aspects of biblical poetics. I see dialogic tension at the heart of the most central and authoritative of biblical genres and voices, that of the law.

Daniel Boyarin and Geoffrey H. Hartman also present a model of biblical discourse that emphasizes simultaneity and difference rather than a sequential, authoritative process. Hartman speaks of the 'frictionality' of Scripture, which

> recalls or should recall the authority of traditions handed down, each with its truth claim—a respect which makes every word, not only the characters, 'schwer von ihrem Gewordensein', to quote Auerbach: heavy with the fullness of having had to be formed.[11]

Boyarin goes further: he finds that conflict is basic to the make-up of the Bible. In his study of the Mekilta, a midrashic collection on the book of Exodus, Boyarin discovers that contradictory rabbinic exegeses of the same passage often actually build on the 'double-voicedness' of the biblical text itself.[12] As an example, Boyarin points to two conflicting opinions concerning the wandering of the Israelites in the desert. R. Yehoshua, who views this as a time of unparalleled closeness between God and Israel, invariably interprets biblical passages in ways that shed a positive light on this period; R. El'azar views the period far more negatively, and this is consistently reflected in his interpretations of the same passages. One of several illustrations

9. I. Pardes, *Countertraditions in the Bible: A Feminist Approach* (Cambridge, MA: Harvard University Press, 1992), p. 4.

10. M. Bal, *Lethal Love: Feminist Literary Readings of Biblical Love Stories* (Bloomington, IN: Indiana University Press, 1987), p. 131.

11. G.H. Hartman, 'The Struggle for Text', in G.H. Hartman and S. Budick (eds.), *Midrash and Literature* (New Haven, CT: Yale University Press, 1986), pp. 13-14.

12. D. Boyarin, *Intertextuality and the Reading of Midrash* (Bloomington, IN: Indiana University Press, 1990), p. 77.

offered by Boyarin is these rabbis' divergent exegesis of the
passage in Exodus (16.3) beginning 'For you have taken us out
into the desert, *to cause this congregation to die of starvation*
[ברעב]'. The Mekilta continues:

> R. Yehoshua says, There is no death which more painful than
> death by starvation, for it says, 'Happier are those who were
> killed by the sword than those killed by hunger' [Lam. 4.9].
> R. El'azar Hammoda'i says, *ba raav* 'Comes starvation': there
> comes upon us starvation upon starvation, plague upon plague,
> darkness upon darkness.[13]

R. Yehoshua tries to minimize the negative aspects of the
Israelites' reaction by ascribing them to their intense and
understandable fear of starvation. R. El'azar, on the other
hand, sees this as the Israelites accusing God of visiting one
catastrophe after another on them, an accusation he finds
outrageous as these are in fact the plagues sent against their
enemies, the Egyptians.

Boyarin points out that these variant readings need not only
reflect the different ideological predispositions of the two
rabbis. They may also be 'a profound response to and doubling
of a tension within the biblical text itself'.[14]

> Built into its very structure is contradiction and opposition. Here
> and all through the canon, there is a dialogue of voices evaluating
> the wilderness period, a voice which proclaims that it was the
> time of greatest love of Israel for her God and a voice which cries
> out that under the very marriage canopy, as it were, Israel was
> unfaithful to her groom.[15]

I think the duality, or multiplicity, of voices which Boyarin so
perceptively notes is mirrored in the role of biblical law in the
literary construction of the Pentateuch. Law contributes to the
biblical polyphony both relationally, in its dialogue with

13. Boyarin, *Intertextuality*, p. 72.
14. Boyarin, *Intertextuality*, p. 75.
15. Boyarin, *Intertextuality*, p. 77. W.L. Reed also discusses biblical multi-
voicedness in his book on Bakhtin and the reading of the Bible: 'The conflict
of interpretations that the critic of the Bible faces may be understood as a
symptom of struggles acted out within the text'. W.L. Reed, *Dialogues of the
Word: The Bible as Literature according to Bakhtin* (New York: Oxford
University Press, 1993), p. 15.

narrative, and intrinsically, in the tensions contained within itself.

If, as Boyarin states, 'contradiction and opposition' are normative to biblical discourse, then the multiplicity of its sources—E, J, D, P—ceases to be simply a quarry for excavation and becomes both evidence of and material for an analysis of biblical polyphony. Why has the redacted text come down to us with its different sources so glaringly visible rather than suppressed? How can one explain the persistent inconsistencies, repetitions, contradictions, and stylistic differences? How are we—as Josipovici so aptly puts it—to 'understand what that putting together might imply'?[16]

I contend that there is a basic impulse towards polyphony in the Bible. This is manifested not only in the visibility of its composite origins but also in the deliberate use of generic heterogeneity. A comprehensive study of the interaction between the various genres in the Bible would be a vast undertaking, so I will focus particularly on law as it relates to narrative. Scholars have largely overlooked the role of law in the biblical polyphony but it merits attention because law, as the linguistic enactment of God's will, encapsulates the grand biblical scheme which attempts to maintain the tension among profoundly conflicting visions of the divine experiment with creation.

Fokkelman's claim that 'the enactments of God are purposefully embedded' is both a comment on biblical poetic typology and a gloss on the linguistic make-up of law as act of communication. Legal texts cannot appear in some 'pure' generic form—even though 'God's enactments' are solely verbal, no one genre can contain them, not even divine law. The legal text, as communicative utterance, must therefore be 'purposefully embedded' in 'fruitful interactions' with a narrative that is in itself unstable and which often undermines the law or is undermined by it. Within the biblical system, law is necessarily part of the chaotic human realm and so 'contaminated'; law cannot remain pure and unmediated revelation. Instead, it becomes the very locus of the ambiguity that pervades biblical theology.

16. Josipovici, *Book of God*, p. 92.

One very interesting communicative aspect of biblical law is expressed in the critical concept of dialogic tension. As Todorov argues in his book on Bakhtin: 'The utterance is not the business of the speaker alone, but the result of his or her interaction with a listener, whose reactions he or she integrates in advance'.[17] The anticipated reaction to, and violation of, the law by the Israelite community is integrated into the text and this is indeed a hallmark of biblical polyphony. For example, the people are incapable of accepting divine law as God's direct speech at Sinai (Exod. 20.16)—the primary legal pronouncement of the whole biblical enterprise—and even as Moses is receiving the law on top of the mountain, the nation below is disobeying it. My analysis demonstrates how the language and structure of the legal material surrounding the Decalogue reveal a profound and pervasive ambivalence.

My treatment of biblical law as ambivalent, embedded communication is based on a larger, anti-essentialist approach to genre in general, and to legal discourse in particular. In this view, law is defined functionally as an act in which the words uttered communicate certain intentions to a community but the act is not complete until the listeners fulfill the instructions, injunctions, etc. that constitute those laws.[18] Thus, the community is both receiver and realizer of the law, the very condition of its constitution.

From this perspective, law of any sort, as the product of a given community, would leave traces of the multiplicity of opinions and voices existing within that community. This is true particularly of biblical law, which functions on a set of rules set

---

17. T. Todorov, *Mikhail Bakhtin: The Dialogical Principle* (trans. W. Godzich; Minneapolis, MN: University of Minnesota Press, 1984), p. 43.

18. This resembles the concept of constitutive rule which Searle discusses in the context of his distinction between institutional facts and brute facts. Brute facts relate to concrete objects governed by the rules of nature, institutional facts are rules set up by the community.

> Every institutional fact is underlain by a (system of) rule(s) of the form 'X counts as Y in context of C'. Our hypothesis that speaking a language is performing acts according to constitutive rules involves us in the hypothesis that the fact that a man performed a certain speech act, e.g., made a promise, is an institutional fact (J.R. Searle, *Speech Acts: An Essay in the Philosophy of Language* [Cambridge: Cambridge University Press, 1969], pp. 50-53).

up by the community and is in some ways constitutive of that community.[19]

From the biblical perspective, being a member of God's covenanted community means living according to that community's laws as set down in its sacred texts. And because law is central to the self-definition of the Israelite community, it contains the ambivalences, the multiplicity of voices, and the complexities of that community. For example, while the command 'you shall not murder' (Exod. 20.13) is an unequivocal prohibition against the unlawful taking of human life, the context clearly includes the presupposition that murder exists in biblical society. Indeed, the prohibition obliquely acknowledges within its own polyphonic structure that in appropriate contexts the taking of human life can actually be a command;[20] the Israelites, for example, are ordered by God to annihilate the Canaanites and the Amalekites (Deut. 7.24; 25.17-19).[21]

19. To demonstrate the difference between constitutive and regulative law, Robert Cover points to Joseph Caro's attempt to bridge two aphorisms, one by Simeon the Just and the other by Rabbi Simeon ben Gamaliel. The former 'creates the normative worlds in which law is predominantly a system of meaning rather than an imposition of force', the latter is 'essentially system-maintaining' ('Nomos and Narrative', pp. 19-25).

20. Nahum Sarna points out that the Hebrew stem רצח 'applies only to illegal killing, and unlike other verbs for the taking of life, is never used in the administration of justice or for killing in war. Also it is never employed when the subject of the action is God or an angel' (N.M. Sarna, *Exodus* [The JPS Torah Commentary; Philadelphia: Jewish Publication Society, 1991], p. 113). To some degree this reading smooths over the contradiction between the prohibition against murder on the one hand, and the fact that in some situations in the Bible the Israelites are not only permitted to shed human blood but even enjoined to do so. Sarna fails to note the polyphonic structure of the biblical text, in which there is a continuing dialectic between the particularistic voice, which focuses almost entirely on Israelite national interests, and the universalistic voice, which expresses a concern for humanity as a whole.

21. Mikhail Bakhtin's linguistic approach to 'utterance' or context of enunciation is similar to that of Searle. Bakhtin finds that utterance is the product of the collective: 'Whatever the moment of the utterance expression we may consider, it will always be determined by the real conditions of its uttering, and foremost by the *nearest social situation*'. Biblical law as utterance, therefore, is determined by the 'social situation' of

In attempting to create a human society, the laws become an expression, even an embodiment, of that society. And the laws, like the society, are both functional and flawed. Thus law, as the expression of God's desire to order creation, also embodies and transmits reservations regarding the likelihood of success of this grand design. Law functions paradoxically as both a stabilizing and a destabilizing force.

In my discussion of the poetics of law in the Bible, I rely on the theoretical framework developed by Mikhail M. Bakhtin[22] whose ground-breaking work on the composite nature of the novel combined with his study of the 'polyphonic novel' has proven useful far beyond the confines of the theory of fiction. In puncturing principles of organic unity in the novel, Bakhtin has presented us with a model for other genres as well. In his essay 'Discourse in the Novel',[23] he states:

> The novel as a whole is a phenomenon multiform in style and variform in speech and voice. In it the investigator is confronted with several heterogeneous stylistic unities, often located on different levels and subject to different stylistic controls.[24]

Bakhtin sees the novel as a heteroglot text, in which diverse voices and genres coexist—not necessarily in harmony. As a result of this 'simultaneity' in which 'everything coexists', the novel achieves meaning not so much through the unfolding of plot as through the dialogic interaction and tension among its

the ancient Israelite community that produced it and reflects its tensions. This quote is cited in Todorov, *The Dialogical Principle*, p. 43; it is from a translation of Bakhtin's 1929 article 'Marxism and the Philosophy of Language' (English version 1973).

22. R. Polzin was the first Bible critic to apply Bakhtin in a literary analysis of the biblical text. See his *Moses and the Deuteronomist: A Literary Study of Deuteronomic History*. Part I. *Deuteronomy, Joshua, Judges* (New York: Seabury Press, 1980). M.M. Bakhtin, *The Dialogic Imagination* (trans. C. Emerson and M. Holquist; Austin, TX: University of Texas Press, 1981). This work is a collection of essays originally published in Russian in the 1930s. See also, M.M. Bakhtin, *Problems of Dostoevsky's Poetics* (ed. and trans. C. Emerson; Minneapolis, MN: University of Minnesota Press, 1984), originally published in Russian in Moscow in the 1920s.

23. Bakhtin, 'Discourse in the Novel', in *The Dialogic Imagination*, pp. 259-422. Originally published in Russian in 1934–1935.

24. 'Discourse in the Novel', p. 261.

various components. Dostoevsky—Bakhtin's paradigmatic author of the polyphonic text—achieves through such simultaneity a 'plurality of equally authoritative ideological positions and an extreme heterogeneity of material...'[25] This multiplicity involves not only genres—part of a phenomenon he terms 'heteroglossia'—but also voices and ideology, a phenomenon he terms 'polyphony'. On both levels, the emphasis on plurality and difference is highly pertinent to the workings of law in the Bible.

Bakhtin's concept of generic heteroglossia seems particularly appropriate to the intricate intertwining of law and narrative in the Bible. Genre for Bakhtin is not a fixed construct, but fluid and functionally defined, always to be viewed in terms of its communicative purposes.[26] Thus genre can fulfill many different roles depending on the context and on the different 'languages' with which it is interacting.

The novel permits the incorporation of various genres, both artistic (short stories, lyrical songs, poems) and extra-artistic (everyday, rhetorical, scholarly, religious genres). All these genres, as they enter the novel, bring into it their own

25. *Dostoevsky's Poetics*, p. 18. Ironically, Bakhtin himself saw the Bible as a monolithic text and would thus have found, in the words of the Slavic literary scholar, M. Holquist, that 'the Bible could never represent the novel in contrast to the epic, since *both*, Bible and epic, would share a presumption of authority, a claim to absolute language, utterly foreign to the novel's joyous awareness of the inadequacies of its own language' (*The Dialogic Imagination*, 'Introduction', p. xxxiii). Harold Fisch also notes that 'In Dostoevsky he [Bakhtin] finds "polyphony"; in *Don Quixote* he finds double-voiced, internally dialogized discourse. But Bakhtin found nothing like this in the Bible; instead he found a univocal discourse quite unlike the "polyphonic" story-telling of Dostoevsky' (H. Fisch, 'Bakhtin's Misreadings of the Bible', *Hebrew University Studies in Literature and the Arts* 16 [1988], p. 139). It would seem that where the Bible is concerned, one must first refute Bakhtin in order to apply him.

26. See especially 'The Problem of Speech Genres', in *M.M. Bakhtin: Speech Genres and Other Late Essays* (trans. V.W. McGee; Austin, TX: University of Texas Press, 1986), pp. 60-102. This essay was originally published in Russia in 1952–1953.

languages, and therefore stratify the linguistic unity of the novel and further intensify its speech diversity in fresh ways.[27]

Elsewhere Bakhtin writes,

> Special emphasis should be placed on the extreme heterogeneity of speech genres (oral and written).[28]

Just so with law in the Bible: rather than understanding it from an essentialist framework which sees law primarily as a stabilizing, conservative force, I understand it as having a multiplicity of roles; a multiplicity expressed in the way law interacts with its narrative context.

Bakhtin's concept of polyphony has proved very useful in uncovering the 'multi-voicedness' within biblical law itself. Polyphony makes audible—visible, in Bakhtin's synesthetic metaphor—many different and even contradictory subject-positions within the novel, positions that are 'presented not within a single field of vision but within several fields of vision, each full of equal worth'.[29] Furthermore, these different visions interact with each other dialogically without smoothing over their differences. Of such interaction in Dostoevsky, Bakhtin says:

> We are dealing here with an ultimate dialogicality, that is, a dialogicality of the ultimate whole...It is constructed not as the whole of a single consciousness, absorbing other consciousnesses as objects into itself, but as a whole formed by the interaction of several consciousnesses, none of which entirely becomes an object for the other.[30]

Dostoevsky's novels thus become, for Bakhtin and many of his followers, the model for discursive practices which are defined by the diversity of genres and voices tensely conjoined within them. These various strata maintain among themselves a dialogic disharmony that causes a dynamic 'where centrifugal as well as centripetal forces are brought to bear'.[31] In this sense, I would claim—with Pardes—that the Bible is 'a paradigmatic case

27. 'Discourse in the Novel', pp. 320-21.
28. 'Problem of Speech Genres', p. 60.
29. *Dostoevsky's Poetics*, p. 16.
30. *Dostoevsky's Poetics*, p. 18.
31. 'Discourse in the Novel', p. 272.

of a Bakhtinian heteroglot text, in which centripetal and centrifugal forces clash with great force'.[32] It is composed of diverse genres, voices, and sociolects that have deliberately been left unharmonized.[33] One might even say that in the Bible multiplicity becomes a kind of ethical—and esthetic—principle. In using Bakhtin's model, it is possible to highlight two types of diversity within the articulation of biblical law: one relates to biblical law as a genre intermingled with other discursive strata that are equally 'impure'; the other focuses on the polyphonic tension built into the very locus of monotheistic authority, biblical law itself.

32. Pardes, *Countertraditions*, p. 122.
33. For a further discussion of a Bakhtinian reading of the Bible see Reed, *Dialogues of the Word*, chapter 1.

Chapter 2

CREATION: MANDATE AND PROHIBITION

The imperfect is our paradise.
Wallace Stevens[1]

My analysis of the interconnection between biblical foundational narratives and law begins with the creation story. Bible scholars and literary critics have often discussed the two quite distinct versions of this story (Gen. 1.1–2.4a; 2.4b-24). The first, attributed to P, depicts creation from the cosmic perspective; the second, attributed to J, focuses primarily on the development of human civilization. Several critics have provided imaginative and innovative readings of the interaction between the two versions: Robert Alter has pointed to the 'composite artistry' evident in the interplay between them; Mieke Bal and Ilana Pardes, among others, analyze the two creation stories from a feminist perspective; David Biale and Daniel Boyarin examine them in their studies on fertility and sexuality in the Bible.[2] My study of this material has a different focus: it examines the divine directives embedded in each of the two versions of creation and analyzes the manner in which they interact with the narratives and with each other.

The two creation stories not only differ in content but seem to be fundamentally at odds, and their conflicting worldviews are reflected in the legal injunctions contained in each: in diction,

1.   W. Stevens, 'The Poems of Our Climate', in *The Palm at the End of the Mind: Selected Poems* (ed. H. Stevens; New York: Vintage Books, 1972 [1967]), p. 158.

2.   R. Alter, *The Art of Biblical Narrative* (New York: Basic Books, 1981), pp. 141-47; Pardes, *Countertraditions*, chs. 2 and 3; Bal, *Lethal Love*; Biale, *Eros and the Jews*, ch. 1; and D. Boyarin, *Carnal Israel: Reading Sex in Talmudic Culture* (Berkeley: University of California Press, 1993).

structure, and placement in the narrative, these encapsulate the vision of creation that dominates the version in which they appear. The first version is consistently holistic in its outlook; the impetus—thematically, stylistically, and linguistically—is to present a creation in which all the pieces are linked in one grand vision of the cosmos.[3] The second version presents a partitive view in its theme and structure; it focuses on a vision of the divine experiment with creation dominated by fragmentation and alienation. In this version, God must share center stage with the humans that he creates but cannot completely control. The tensions in this second creation story foreshadow the strife that will, from the biblical perspective, characterize the divine–human relationship.

Although I refer to the Priestly (P) version of creation as the first account and the Yahwist (J) version as the second, the scholarly consensus is that the J version in fact predates P. However, even if the version appearing first in the extant biblical text was composed long after the second and reflects a different and more harmonious theology, the point at issue here is the way in which the two interact. The Priestly writers did not, after all, simply delete the existing story and replace it with their own. This may be partly because that account had the authority of antiquity; but it may well be, too, that these writers had an intuitive sense (in keeping with the general functioning of law in the Bible) that their harmonizing version of creation and its first injunction to humanity—'Be fruitful and increase'— should interact dialectically with the other version. The Priestly writers may have felt the need to moderate the division and conflict that dominate the Eden story, but the fact that they retained it indicates that the partitive vision is basic to biblical theology.

The dichotomy between the two versions of creation is highlighted in the divine legal pronouncements which each one contains. The first legal mandate in the Bible appears at the

---

3.   Unless otherwise indicated, I will be citing biblical passages in English translation from the *Tanakh: A New Translation of the Holy Scriptures according to the Traditional Hebrew Text* (Philadelphia: Jewish Publication Society, 1985).

conclusion of the first version of creation. The passage offers a
retrospective condensation of the full scope of creation:

> God blessed them and God said to them, 'Be fertile and increase,
> fill the earth and master it; and rule the fish of the sea, the birds of
> the sky, and all living things that creep on the earth'. God said,
> 'See, I give you every seed-bearing plant that is upon all the
> earth, and every tree that has seed-bearing fruit; they shall be
> yours for food. And to all the animals on land, to all the birds of
> the sky, and to everything that creeps on earth, in which there is
> the breath of life, [I give] all the green plants for food'. And so it
> was (1.28-30).

In trying to enumerate the manifold aspects of life which have
just been brought into being, the mandate presents an
overview, a checklist of sorts, of the entire enterprise, and
functions as a culmination of its holistic impulse.

The sense of inclusiveness that characterizes the first version
is heightened by the repeated use of the word כל ('every' or
'all'). It first appears in v. 21 in reference to the creation of the
sea-dwelling creatures, reappears in the narrative with greater
and greater frequency as the full range of species is brought
into being, and reaches a crescendo in the language of the
divine mandate. The momentum built by the incremental
repetition of כל augments the sense of an authoritative, directed
coalescence, and helps create the vision of a vast assemblage of
diverse elements made to cohere into a unified whole:

ויאמר אלהים הנה נתתי לכם את־כל־עשב זרע זרע אשר על־פני כל־
הארץ ואת־כל־העץ אשר־בו פרי־עץ זרע זרע לכם יהיה לאכלה
ולכל־חית הארץ ולכל־עוף השמים ולכל רומש על־הארץ אשר־בו נפש
חיה את־כל־ירק עשב לאכלה ויהי־כן וירא אלהים את־כל־אשר עשה
והנה־טוב מאד (1.29-31a)

This vision sets the stage for the final use of כל, which appears
in the verse that follows the legal text: וירא אלהים את־כל־אשר עשה
והנה־טוב מאד ('And God saw all that he had made, and found it
very good') (1.31). All of creation having been assembled in the
mandate, God takes one last all-encompassing view and finds it
'very good'.

This momentum towards inclusiveness is reinforced further by
the rapid sequence of imperative verbs that begins the divine
charge: פרו ורבו ומלאו את־הארץ וכבשה ורדו בדגת הים ('Be fertile,

increase and fill the earth and master it; and rule the fish of the sea'). The verbs build in rhythmic intensity as they progress in quick succession from fertility, which represents life in its potential state, to dominion, which represents human life in its most realized and active form and which is the most god-like of all human activities.[4] As with the repetitive use of כל, this compact catalogue of verbs mirrors linguistically the dense assemblage of the first creation story.

A further indication of the holistic impulse of the mandate is the way it recombines materials from earlier in the narrative. It weaves the blessing of fertility bestowed on the birds and sea creatures (1.22) with God's speech concerning the creation of man and woman (1.26), thus bringing two distinct speeches into a single, all-encompassing address. The text here is heteroglot in an almost literal sense: this is combined, divine speech, and law is its locus. The linguistic nature of the act of creation is thereby underscored by the verbal nature of the mandate as the ultimate form of divine address. Thus law, too, is created in the creation story. Whereas each speech in the mandate is concerned with a different particular stage of creation, animal and human, the final mandate integrates them into a unified whole. This integration also mitigates somewhat the potential adversarial nature between the two different life forms. Although the verbs כבשה ('master') and רדו ('rule') can be understood as menacing, in the context of the divine mandate they represent one aspect of a larger picture, a picture that is ordered by a consistent authority and remains harmonious even as the threatening connotations of these terms loom in the background.

Just as the mandate depicts the relationship between human and animal life as balanced and ordered, so too does it draw on the relationship between God and humanity. In the arrangement God makes with man and woman concerning the governance of the new entity he has brought into being, he de-emphasizes his own dominance and places the unbounded scope

---

4. One might view procreation (פרו ורבו), too, as a godlike activity in that it is the human counterpart to the divine creation בצלם אלהים ('in the image of God'). However, the animal world is also commanded to be fruitful and increase (1.23) while only humans have a mandate to rule.

and freedom of human activity in the foreground. As beings created in his own image, God delegates to humans an aspect of his life-giving powers and a portion of his sovereignty. This lack of rigid stratification is also extended to the relationship between man and woman: the mandate empowers both, and does not seem to distinguish between them on any grounds.[5] The mandate thus binds all elements of creation, from plants and animals to the divine, in a series of harmonious and interlocking relationships that suggest unity and equality even while asserting authority and domination.

The balanced nature of this creation story is also seen in the blurring of the lines between law and blessing in the פרו ורבו section. God's enunciation of this mandate can be seen as a speech act of blessing, ויברך אתם ('and he blessed them'), but the articulated semantic content is that of command. After creating man and woman, God does not continue to be a direct participant in procreation but charges humanity with that responsibility. The deity grants humanity the privilege of populating the world and ruling it, but in the form of a charge: human beings are the *agents* for enacting God's blessing; they are accountable to God in fulfilling this obligation.[6]

A similar blurring of blessing and command recurs in the Noahide laws (9.1-8): in v. 1 God's speech act is both a charge and a blessing, ויברך אלהים את־נח ואת־בניו ויאמר להם פרו ורבו ומלאו את־הארץ ('God blessed Noah and his sons, and said to them, "Be fertile and increase, and fill the earth"'). In the restatement of the mandate (v. 7), however, the performative verb ברך is absent, and the imperative aspect predominates: ואתם פרו ורבו שרצו בארץ ורבו־בה ('And as for you, be fertile and increase; abound on the earth and increase on it').[7] Thus while v. 1 seems to repeat the first creation story, v. 7 is a much diminished

---

5. See Pardes, *Countertraditions*, Chapter 3: 'Creation According to Eve'; P. Trible, 'Clues in the Text', in *God and the Rhetoric of Sexuality* (Philadelphia: Fortress Press, 1978); and Bal, *Lethal Love*, chapter 5: 'Sexuality, Sin, and Sorrow'.

6. The verbs 'bless' and 'command' actually appear together in Gen. 28.1 where Isaac blesses Jacob and commands him to go Paddan-aram to find a wife (ויברך אתו ויצוהו).

7. My translation.

version: primarily a list of commands (especially with the emphatic use of the personal pronoun ואתם—literally 'and you [plural]'—to introduce the imperative). Indeed, the fact that the divine mandate of 'be fertile and increase' appears without the introductory ויברך אתם in that instance emphasizes the degree to which God has distanced himself from a humanity that has betrayed its charge and has already proven itself capable of destroying life (see Chapter 3).[8]

The divine charge of the first creation story thus seems to effect a grand resolution, perhaps even a stasis. This would hardly conform to my thesis that there also exists an undermining element in biblical law. But, in fact, the composite whole that has been created by the juxtaposition of the two creation stories results, as I will presently demonstrate, in a dialogic tension and even friction within the biblical text which is ultimately left unharmonized.

Injunctions to be fertile, proliferate, and take nourishment form the basis of human empowerment in the divine mandate of the first creation account; these very elements, however, become the core of the struggle between humanity and God in the legal prohibition of the second version. While repetition is the crucial vehicle of linguistic unity in the first account,

---

8.　The legal significance of the divine injunction to 'be fertile and increase' is not recorded until the talmudic period. There are indications in the Bible, however, that it was considered an obligation in biblical times as well, and that those who disobeyed the charge of procreation were severely punished. Onan apparently dies because he disregarded the divine mandate (Gen. 38.9-11). Not only did he spill his seed expressly to avoid bringing forth new life, but in so doing he was also refusing to fulfill his responsibility as a levir: the obligation to keep the name of his dead brother alive by impregnating his widow. Indeed, the biblical condemnation of most forms of non-procreative sexuality, including the death penalty for homosexuality (Lev. 20.13) can also be understood as punishment for violating the divine mandate to be fertile and increase. Boyarin says that 'reproduction was a site of central, vital significance in the rabbinic culture, with genealogy serving as a crucial source of meaning' (*Carnal Israel*, p. 198). This concern may well be rooted in the biblical world which was the source of rabbinic culture. See Biale, *Eros and the Jews*, chapter 1, and H. Eilberg-Schwartz, *The Savage in Judaism: An Anthropology of Israelite Religion and Ancient Judaism* (Bloomington, IN: Indiana University Press, 1990), chapter 6.

rhetorical paradox is the most salient expressive device in the second:

> And the Lord God commanded the man, saying, 'Of every tree of the garden you are free to eat; but as for the tree of knowledge of good and bad, you must not eat of it; for as soon as you eat of it, you shall die' (2.16-17).

The destabilizing qualities of the prohibition are apparent both in its rhetoric and in its insertion in the narrative just before the creation of Eve. It begins with an affirmative statement that appears to echo the permissive holism of the first mandate. But here the כל of 'every tree' is a syntactic illusion: it leads to the לא תאכל ('you must not eat') of the excluded, forbidden tree. The last phrase is a contradiction of the first, creating a rhetorical dynamic of permission and restraint that undermines the initial message. Food no longer represents God's expansiveness alone; it is also emblematic of a power and dominion that are exclusively his.

The dynamic tension between giving and withdrawing is also reproduced structurally in the interaction between the two divine statements of ch. 1 and ch. 2. The charge 'be fertile and increase' (פרו ורבו), the grant of dominion, and the permission to eat of everything—all essential elements of the first account—go unmentioned here. The word מכל, with its expansive, holistic connotations, gives way to לא ('no, not'): לא תאכל ממנו ('you must not eat of it'). Indeed, the negation לא dominates the second account just as surely as כל dominated the first, and it highlights the limiting, partitive vision of this anthropocentric, earth-bound version of creation.

The partitive nature of the injunction is further reflected in the way it is positioned in the narrative. It does not appear at the very end of the account of creation, as does the divine mandate of the first version, but instead before the animals or Eve come into being. The injunction thus disrupts the flow of the account and places a wedge between its key figures: placing the prohibition before Eve is created sets up a fundamental tension which was not present in the narrative before. Man, woman, and God are no longer one unified but complex entity; they are set apart from one another in a way that highlights the struggle and conflict that lie at the core of the vision of the second creation story. The prohibition thus does not merely limit human freedom to act, but shatters the holistic vision of creation. Paradoxically, even God's dominion is diminished: though the injunction ostensibly asserts God's absolute power, it in fact results in a challenge to that power. No longer is God the sole active agent, nor are humans a perfect replica of God. From now on, God must share the stage with a creation that has somehow escaped from him, a creation with a will of its own but with only limited ability to act.

Food and sexual activity are linked in both legal pronouncements in ways that further highlight the conflicting visions of creation. In the first narrative, the fulfillment of the charge 'be fertile and increase' is connected to eating of the fruit of the land; eating and eroticism are seamlessly integrated into a perfectly wrought life cycle, the concrete expression of God's beneficence and the means by which he empowers humanity. In the second account, on the other hand, sexual activity and food are used to express God's dominion and power; they are the means by which he sets himself apart from his creation.[9]

This process of separation is extended to relations within creation as well. It is not clear from the text what Adam and Eve actually discover—sexuality or shame—as a result of eating the fruit.[10] Traditional Jewish thought holds that they had sexual relations in the garden of Eden before this time, and the story is not concerned with a 'fall into sexuality'; Christian scholarship, as is well known, differs on this issue.[11] In either

---

9.   Although the tree of knowledge of good and evil is linked explicitly to sexuality only in the post-biblical reception of the Garden of Eden story, a good case can be made that, as far as the legal inserts are concerned, a connection between knowledge and sexuality is suggested within the biblical text itself. The prohibition's insertion into the text immediately before God's decision to create a companion for Adam provides a suggestive circumstantial link between the two. Moreover, the proverbial 'to know in the biblical sense' has its origins in the Adam and Eve narrative: the root יד"ע, used first to describe the tree of knowledge of good and evil (עץ הדעת טוב ורע), then appears in Gen. 4.1 in the first explicit depiction of a sexual act in the Bible: והאדם ידע את־חוה אשתו ('Now the man *knew* his wife Eve').

10. This was suggested to me by Daniel Boyarin.

11. See Boyarin, *Carnal Israel*, chapter 3; I. Pardes, 'Beyond Genesis 3',

case, however, the linking of food and sexuality in the divine legal pronouncement of the second creation story brings about a separation, even a rupture, among all the parties which provides a stark contrast to the nurturing cohesiveness implied in the mandate of the first.[12] Indeed, the association of sexuality with food in the prohibition entails the very opposite of nurturing, namely death: 'You must not eat of it; for as soon as you eat of it, you shall die'. Food and sex do not lead here to empowerment and blessing but to a three-way connection between knowledge, sexuality, and mortality.

The two versions of creation can also be contrasted in terms of the treatment of the mandates. In the first version, God is both addresser and addressee, agent and receiver of the speech acts of creation. This speech need not be directed at anyone; it is holistically self-contained and self-fulfilling: 'God said, "let there be x"' is followed immediately, automatically by 'and there was x' (or 'and it was so'), a formulaic description of success. God's speech creates reality; his actions become their own realization. Even the mandate of fertility and dominion, פרו ורבו—the highpoint of the divine flow—is followed by the statement 'And it was so' (1.30). And the entire series of creation pronouncements is followed by an account of God's survey: 'And God saw all that He had made, and found it very good' (1.31). The enactment of law is thus plenitude and goodness. God's unmediated, non-communicative speech is an expression of the holism of his creation.

In the partitive second version, by contrast, addresser and addressee are quite separate entities. This results in impaired channels of communication, as God's utterances go unheeded

Hebrew University Studies in Literature and the Arts 17 (1989), pp. 161-87; G. Anderson, 'Celibacy or Consummation in the Garden of Eden? Reflections on Early Jewish and Christian Interpretations of the Garden of Eden', *HTR* 82.2 (1989), pp. 121-48.

12. My reading thus differs from that of traditional rabbinic exegesis, which sees the Garden of Eden as a 'concentrated locus of divine blessing—a blessing which actualizes itself in sexual fertility' (Anderson, 'Celibacy or Consummation', p. 139). To arrive at such an understanding of the Eden story, it seems to me, the ancient Jewish exegetes had to skirt the tension and conflict that is at the core of the narrative and its injunction, and view it through the prism of the first account of creation.

and therefore unenacted. What is more, the divine speech itself is disruptive and destabilizing: in contrast to the seamless flow between act and effect in the first mandate, the legal speech here communicates discontinuity, even friction; it becomes part of the divisiveness that characterizes this version of creation. Even as God utters the injunction 'you must not eat of it' he is creating the conditions which result in a divergence of effect from act. The injunction is partitive not only because it abruptly introduces direct speech into third-person narrative, but also in its ambivalence concerning the full realization of this mandate, a realization that requires the listener—namely the first human— to fulfill its instructions.

Addresser and addressee are one and the same in the mandate of the first creation story; in the second the addressee becomes more and more removed from addresser. In fact, a counter-embedded speech on the part of the addressee— represented by the serpent—deliberately attempts to subvert the speech of the addresser. The gulf between act and effect in the second creation story thus highlights its partitive impulse, just as the harmoniousness between act and effect reflect the holistic impulse of the first.

Chapter 3

THE LAW OF THE FLOOD:
BETWEEN DECREATION AND RECREATION

The narrative of Noah and the flood is closely linked to the two creation stories and alludes to them in both its narrative and legal content. The Noah story also depicts a major rupture in divine–human relations, yet exile is no longer sufficient punishment. Humanity has become so depraved that God resolves to annihilate that which he has created. However, he cannot bring himself to destroy completely what he had crafted with so much care and pleasure, and so he preserves enough of it to begin anew. The eventual success of this second attempt at creation, however, is called into question from the very start. Alongside hope for renewal, the narrative also presents a highly pessimistic message. This instability in the narrative is mirrored in the legal insert at its core (9.1-7). The divine laws against murder embedded in the text reinforce the subversive themes of the narrative both in texture and in structure.

That the Noah story is also a creation story is clear from the echoing in 9.1 of the divine mandate found in the first version of creation: 'God blessed Noah and his sons, and said to them, "Be fertile and increase, and fill the earth"'. However, the laws that follow soon make it clear that this is a creation story of a different order from the first. The reconstitution of life after the flood does not mean a return to the harmony of the first account of creation. Indeed, the divine charge of fertility in the context of the post-diluvian era takes on a bitter double meaning, for the flood narrative may be better understood as a 'decreation' story in which God reverses the processes that he himself had set in motion:

> When the waters had swelled much more upon the earth, all the
> highest mountains everywhere under the sky were covered. And
> all flesh that stirred on earth perished—birds, cattle, beasts, and
> all the things that swarmed upon the earth, and all mankind (7.19,
> 21).

The destruction of life closely parallels the order of its creation
as recounted in the first creation story:

> God said, 'Let the earth bring forth swarms of living creatures,
> and birds that fly above the expanse of the sky.' God said, 'Let the
> earth bring forth every kind of living creature: cattle, creeping
> things, and wild beasts of every kind' (1.20, 24).

As it is placed immediately after the narrative of the diluvian
destruction, the repetition of the primeval injunction 'be fertile
and increase' functions both to reiterate and to counter-balance
the narrative. The legal material is thus organized within a
contrapuntal structure where the statement of the theme
(creation) is followed by its reversal (deterioration culminating
in the flood) which in turn is followed by a repetition of the
original theme (creation).

In one sense, then, the use of פרו ורבו as a frame functions as a
divine reaffirmation of life and a note of promise and hope. At
the same time, the repetition of the primordial mandate to Noah
and his family exposes how much has changed since it was first
uttered. פרו ורבו now reverberates with the urgency of survival;
it is law as a crucial measure aimed literally at filling (מלאו) a
near-empty earth. There is no sense of unequivocal celebration
in this renewed charge, only resignation on the part of the deity
facing the reality of an imperfect world: '...and the Lord said to
Himself: "Never again will I curse the earth because of man,
since the devisings of man's mind are evil from his youth..."'
(8.21). The divine mandate in its new context represents God's
willingness to renew his relationship with humanity, but not
necessarily his approbation or even trust. In its structural
interaction with the narrative material, the legal injunction פרו
ורבו paradoxically stresses in its very reiteration the dialogic,
heteroglot nature of this major liminal moment. It not only calls
into play the role of God as creator of the universe but also his
role as its destroyer.

The divine charge of procreation also enters into ambivalent rapport with the laws that it frames: a series of laws that are fundamentally in conflict with the charge of fertility, cast it in a highly ironic light, and thereby call into question its very possibility or indeed desirability. If פרו ורבו harks back to the first version of creation, these laws abruptly deflect the focus to the second version, where the themes of alienation and estrangement are dominant. The introductory charge of procreation to Noah (9.1) continues as follows:

> The fear and dread of you shall be upon all the beasts of the earth and upon all the birds of the sky...Every creature that lives shall be yours to eat...You must not, however, eat flesh with its life-blood in it (אך־בשר בנפשו דמו לא תאכלו) (9.2-4).

This allusive repetition of the original command to procreate remains in unresolved tension with the text's further allusion, in v. 5 ('I will require it of every beast'), to the punishment inflicted on the serpent for causing the violation of the prohibition against eating the fruit of the tree of knowledge. God curses the serpent in the second creation story by decreeing a permanent state of hostility between it and humanity:

> Because you did this
> More cursed shall you be
> Than all cattle
> And all the wild beasts:
> On your belly you shall crawl
> And dirt shall you eat
> All the days of your life.
> I will put enmity
> Between you and the woman
> And between your offspring and hers;
> They shall strike at your head,
> And you shall strike at their heel (3.14-15).

Thus animal and human are set against each other in eternal conflict in punishment for the failure of both to abide by the law. It is this discord which is intertextually echoed in the 'fear and dread' (מוראכם וחתכם) of God's charge of dominion to Noah (9.2): 'The fear and dread of you shall be upon all the beasts of the earth and upon all the birds of the sky—everything with which the earth is astir—and upon all the fish of the sea...' The injunction in the Noahide law emphasizes the state of perpetual antagonism that God decreed between humanity and the environment it was empowered by God to rule.[1]

The primordial charge emphasized human power: '...fill the earth and master it (וכבשה); and rule (ורדו) the fish of the sea, etc.', yet downplayed the association between this dominion and the destructive potential of those exercising power. The flood story, by contrast, demonstrates how human conduct can bring about the devastation of nature and the realization of God's curse. Therefore, just as the Noahide decrees allusively recapitulate the two primordial laws, פרו ורבו and לא תאכל ממנו ('you must not eat of it')—laws which are tensely dialogic in themselves—they also add a new ambivalence, the destructive potential of human power, to the biblical textual polyphony.

In the verses that follow, the theme of 'fear and dread' is extended beyond nature's reaction to humanity to the realm of human affairs. This shift occurs through the stark, even startling, insertion of a dietary law, transforming the ground from domination to consumption. Like the first decree to Noah,

---

1.   Speiser's translation of מוראכם וחתכם as 'Dread fear of you shall possess all the animals of the earth...' (*Genesis* [AB; Garden City, NY: Doubleday, 1964], p. 57) further emphasizes the relationship as an antagonistic one. This is a hendiadys that recurs with slight differences in Deut. 11.25, and in verbal form in Deut. 1.21, 31.8. Interestingly, most commentators do not note the threatening, antagonistic implications of this expression. The hendiadys in Deut. 11.25 occurs in the context of the fear that will strike the native populations of Canaan at the sight of the invading Israelites: 'No man shall stand up to you: the Lord your God will put the *dread and the fear of you* (פחדכם ומוראכם) over the whole land in which you set foot, as He promised you'.

By contrast, Cassuto's reading of Gen. 9.2, actually takes the passage as an affirmation of humanity:

> This attitude of fear and dread may be due to the fact that the creatures were saved from the Flood on account of man and through his action; from now on they would realize more clearly the superiority of the human species. (U. Cassuto, *A Commentary on the Book of Genesis*. II. *From Noah to Abraham* [Jerusalem: Magnes Press, 1964], p. 125.)

Cassuto seems to be harking back to the original appearance of this command of dominion, maintaining the holistic stance of the first version of creation. I find the text presents a far more ambivalent and cautious vision of humanity.

this law seems to mirror the mandate in the first creation story, yet at the same time allude to the dietary prohibition of the second. At first, the holistic emphasis on total permission appears to dominate: 'Every creature that lives shall be yours to eat; as with the green grasses, I give you all these' (9.3). A further link to the mandate of the first creation story is the repetition of the word כל which appears six times in vv. 2-3, echoing 1.28-31, where the repetition represented coherence and unity. However here, with the discussion of eating meat, there is an abrupt shift to the partitive, restrictive perspective of the second version of creation: 'You must not, however, eat flesh with its life-blood in it' (9.4). This prohibition further elaborates on the 'fear and dread' that will henceforth define the relationship between the animal and the human world, intensifying the sense of conflict between the two domains that was already an element in their relationship in the second creation story.

The Noahide mandate thus reiterates and reinforces the dialogic tension present in the interaction between the legal aspects of the two creation stories. The laws of the post-diluvian 'recreation' of the world do not resolve the clash between the two profoundly different biblical visions of creation, but rather put the contrast into even sharper focus.

This friction is also reflected on a structural level, in the interaction between the laws and the narrative in which they are embedded. The transition in the Noahide law from the blessing of procreation to the prohibition of murder which lies at its center can be seen as a response to the deterioration of the human condition recounted in the narratives. Murder is introduced at the very beginning of human history with the killing of Abel by Cain, and it is alluded to again in the speech of Lemech to his wives (4.23-24). The degeneration continues with the cohabitation of divine beings and humans and reaches its lowest point with Noah's generation:

When God saw how corrupt the earth was, for all flesh had corrupted its ways on earth, God said to Noah, 'I have decided to put an end to all flesh, for the earth is filled with lawlessness (חמס) because of them: I am about to destroy them with the earth' (6.12-13).

The flood, however, does not really solve God's problems with his unruly creation; it does not result in a chastened and cleansed humanity. The laws reflect this equivocation while at the same time representing a renewed attempt by the deity to deal with this reality. After the deluge, it is not humanity that changes but God. He yields before the realization that '...the devisings of man's mind are evil from his youth...' (יצר לב האדם רע מנעריו) (8.21) and comes to terms with the imperfection of his creation. The giver of the law is here well aware that the channels of communication have been seriously impaired: his action will in all probability not be followed by a satisfactory response. From the biblical perspective, however, divine legal speech acts are the primary mode of communication between God and creation and therefore must be enunciated even if their successful reception is far from assured.

The Noahide laws are articulated in a succession of decrees which reach a crescendo in the poetic statement of the law prohibiting murder (9.6). Rapid delivery heightens the sense of urgency and concern implied in the laws which can be seen as a response to the increasingly flawed nature of human conduct. Just as it focuses our attention on the thematic tensions between plenitude and withdrawal, so this heightened syntactic tempo lays bare the *communicative* aspect of biblical law. This is law as urgent, verbal message, law demanded by the pragmatic context of the social conditions to which it responds. Intensifying this rhetorical urgency is the repetition of the word אך ('but') at the beginning of vv. 4 and 5 (absent in the English translation). As the addresser's concern with the addressee's condition increases, the legal material shifts from an emphasis on life to a preoccupation with death, forming a psychologically compelling chain of linguistic associations:

> Every creature that lives shall be yours to eat;
> as with the green grasses, I give you all these (9.3).
> You must not, however, eat flesh with its life blood in it (9.4).
> But for your own life-blood I will require a
> reckoning: I will require it of every beast; of man
> too, will I require a reckoning for human life, of
> every man for that of his fellow man (9.5).
> Whoever sheds the blood of man,

By man shall his blood be shed;[2]
For in His image
Did God make man (9.6).

שפך דם האדם
באדם דמו ישפך
כי בצלם אלהים
(9.6) עשה את־האדם

The (permitted) consumption of the green grasses flows into the (prohibited) consumption of flesh with its blood which in turn is transformed into the (prohibited) shedding of human blood. The polyphonic tension between the blessing of פרו ורבו on the one hand and 'fear and dread' on the other is thus further developed in the friction between the two parts of the law dealing with food: the act of food consumption, which is life-sustaining is juxtaposed with the human bloodshed that perverts the very idea of food as nurturing life. 'Fear and dread' is no longer merely an aspect of the human interaction with nature alone, but a defining characteristic of human society itself. In the Noahide laws, the concern with food may still echo God's beneficence and expansiveness, but the laws gradually take on menacing overtones as they become associated with humanity's capacity for the taking of life.

The gravity with which the text views the act of murder is highlighted not only in the content of the laws but also in their formulation. The law is articulated first in prose, but it is a prose with repetitions that border on the parallelism of biblical poetry:

ואך את־דמכם לנפשתיכם אדרש
מיד כל־חיה אדרשנו
ומיד האדם מיד איש אחיו
(9.5) אדרש את־נפש האדם

The law does not explicitly forbid killing, but rather describes God's response to such an action. In spite of his deepening estrangement from creation, God still affirms human life and will not tolerate the violation of its sanctity.

Implicit in this law, and indeed in its very form as exhortation and warning, is an immediate, urgent, and direct involvement

2. J. Milgrom translates this as 'For the sake of that person shall his blood be spilled' (*Leviticus* [AB; Garden City, NY: Doubleday, 1992], p. 705).

on the part of God. Both meanings of the verb דרש (אדרשנו) apply here: to hold accountable, and to request or even plead.[3] The divine speaker states unequivocally that any person who sheds the blood of another is accountable directly to him. This immediacy of involvement in calling a killer to account is first demonstrated in the narrative in the deity's words to Cain after he slew Abel: '...Hark, your brother's blood cries out to Me from the ground!' (4.10). The injunction to Noah in ch. 9 alludes to this passage, while broadening its scope from fratricide to a universal prohibition of murder. Repetition of the verb דרש heightens the tension between closeness and distance on the part of the deity that is the focus of this law. On one hand it reflects God's resignation to the fact of an imperfect world which requires laws against murder; on the other it emphasizes God's affirmation of life, which he sees as an extension of himself: 'For in his image did God make man' (9.6). This statement in its present context may itself be considered polyphonically: it alludes to the divine celebration of the first creation story, but juxtaposing this allusion with the law against murder also highlights the fact that the divine nature of creation had been corrupted since humans were first brought into being. If human life was created as a parallel to—or an extension of— God, then the destruction of the human incarnation of the divine, the spilling of human blood, becomes tantamount to deicide in miniature.

The parallelism in 9.5 ascends incrementally up the chain of creation, from plants to the animal world to humanity in general, and concludes with the personal responsibility that human beings have for each other. The phrase מיד איש אחיו can be translated literally as 'man from his brother', which augments the sense that all of humanity is connected, implied in the text. It also emphasizes the allusion to the Cain and Abel story with which this legal passage maintains multiple intertextual relations: what is literal brotherhood there becomes here the figurative familial bond of all humanity.

In terms of genre, the articulation of the law in v. 5, though not itself written entirely in poetic parallelisms, employs

3. See BDB, p. 205.

incremental repetition, a feature typical of biblical poetry.[4] Thus the genre affiliation of this important transitional verse seems deliberately hazy. Its poetic prose allows for a clear statement of the law, while at the same time preparing the ground for the poetic and ethical 'measure for measure' that follows in v. 6: שֹׁפֵךְ דַּם הָאָדָם בָּאָדָם דָּמוֹ יִשָּׁפֵךְ כִּי בְּצֶלֶם אֱלֹהִים עָשָׂה אֶת־הָאָדָם ('Whoever sheds the blood of man, by man shall his blood be shed; for in His image did God make man') (9.6).[5] The alliterative repetition of the syllable *dam* both as morpheme and lexeme brings added emphasis to the law's primary theme by stressing the physical and moral interconnection of *dām* ('blood') and *ʾadām* ('human'). The pattern of concentric symmetry, abc/cba, offers, as Fokkelman points out, 'a precise image of a balanced legal retribution',[6] that is, the poetic parallelism echoes the ethical balance (מדה כנגד מדה). The concluding statement, 'for in the image of God/made he man', serves to explain the law's motivation and links it to the creation of man and woman in the first creation story: 'And God said, "Let us make man in our image, after our likeness"' (1.27). The contrapuntal flow of creation, decreation, and recreation manifested in the overall interplay of law and narrative in chs. 1–9.7 is thus recapitulated in the interplay of the laws themselves.

פרו ורבו frames chs. 1–9.7, occurring as it does in vv. 1.28 and 9.7, but this selfsame command also serves to frame the Noahide laws alone, recurring in vv. 9.1 and 9.7. This frame within a frame underscores the biblical author's plural attitudes to the human potential for change, both on the level of genre (narrative vs. legal) and on the level of voice (within the legal genre itself). Structurally, the mandate stands in dialogic tension with the narrative it envelops, providing a counter-voice to the pessimistic vision of humanity contained within that narrative.

4. See R. Alter, *The Art of Biblical Poetry* (New York: Basic Books, 1985), chapter 3, 'Structures of Intensification'.
5. The JPS translation adds the word 'God' to the translation of 6b; the Hebrew original does not use God's name. Fokkelman's translation is more accurate: 'for in the image of God/made he man' (J.P. Fokkelman, 'Genesis', in R. Alter and F. Kermode [eds.], *The Literary Guide to the Bible* [Cambridge, MA: Harvard University Press, 1987], p. 45).
6. Fokkelman, 'Genesis', p. 45.

This interaction may be a paradigmatic example of what Bakhtin calls dialogic disharmony between a diversity of genres in a text, a disharmony that causes a dynamic 'where centrifugal as well as centripetal forces are brought to bear'.[7] The mandate of dominion and procreation may temper the grim message of the narrative by enclosing it within the holistic vision of the first creation story; however, the dissonance between the legal frame and its narrative center also colors the way we read the reiterated mandate. As a result of its interaction with the narrative, the post-diluvian divine directive of פרו ורבו is no longer self-contained and self-fulfilling as in the first creation story; the formulaic description 'and so it was' is also not repeated. The recipients of the laws have already shown themselves unwilling to receive the lawgiver's communication. The renewed utterance of the mandate must be read in light of this disrupted communication.

Dialogic tension is further intensified by the ambivalence found within the law itself. The divine mandate, functioning as a frame within a frame, brackets the prohibition against murder— which itself derives from a strongly negative vision of the human condition, a vision that ultimately undermines the mandate's holistic message. The law thus mirrors in its polyphony the friction created by the interplay of law and narrative in the overall account of creation, decreation, and recreation in the book of Genesis. The series concludes as it began, with a reiteration of the primordial mandate: 'Be fertile, then, and increase; abound (שרצו) on the earth and increase (רבו) on it' (9.7).

The passage that directly follows the Noahide laws concerns the establishment of God's covenant, and it, too, reflects the biblical compromise with a reality in which the channels of communication are no longer intact. Divine action and response are again conflated as in the first creation story, but this time the conflation reflects the breakdown of the holistic vision of creation, not its affirmation:

> And God said to Noah and to his sons with him, I now establish
> My covenant with you and your offspring to come, and with

7.   Bakhtin, 'Discourse in the Novel', p. 272. See p. 23, above.

> every living thing that is with you—birds, cattle, and every wild beast as well—all that have come out of the ark, every living thing on earth. I will maintain My covenant with you: never again shall all flesh be cut off by the waters of a flood, and never again shall there be a flood to destroy the earth (9.8-11).

The notion of covenant (ברית) which is so central to God's relationship with Israel is first introduced here.[8] However, whereas the covenant that God concludes with Israel in the book of Exodus is a contractual arrangement involving two parties (Exod. 19; 24.1-11), the covenant in the Noahide account involves only one active party, namely God. God's speech includes the word הנני, a word used in the Bible to emphasize God's determination to act (Gen. 44.4; Exod. 9.18; 34.11) but also as a code-word signaling an individual's willingness to accept the terms of a mandate (Gen. 22.1; 46.2; 1 Sam. 3.4). In the post-diluvian covenant, however, God takes on both roles.[9] The aftermath of the flood does not find improved channels of communication between the divine and the human; rather, God accepts that where the preservation of life on earth is concerned, he alone must function as both agent and recipient of legal pronouncements. In the preceding legal passage God demands that humanity respect the sanctity of life and preserve it; in the covenant with Noah, God takes it upon himself to do the same. The deity repeats in a formal, ritualized, and public promise what had previously been a private locution:

8. Some commentators view the fertility mandate as a covenant; see J. Cohen's discussion (*Be Fertile and Increase, Fill the Earth and Master It: The Ancient and Medieval Career of a Biblical Text* [Ithaca, NY: Cornell University Press, 1989], p. 47). The term ברית, nevertheless, is first used in the biblical text in the Noah story. For a discussion of the concept of ברית in the Bible see D.R. Hillers, *Covenant: The History of a Biblical Idea* (Baltimore, MD: Johns Hopkins University Press, 1969), and K. Baltzer, *The Covenant Formulary in the Old Testament, Jewish and Early Christian Writings* (trans. D.E. Green; Philadelphia: Fortress Press, 1971).

9. Hillers also notes the one-sidedness of this covenant: 'There is no obligation whatever laid on Noah and his descendants, expressed or implied. This is simply a unilateral promise of God, and it makes no difference what Noah does. Even human corruption will not change it...' (*Covenant*, pp. 101-102).

> So long as the earth endures
> Seedtime and harvest
> Cold and heat
> Summer and Winter
> Day and Night
> Shall not cease (8.21-22).

This is not intended to elicit a response. Rather, the covenant takes the form of a promise. For life to continue, God's dictum must be its own realization. Through the covenant, cosmic order is restored, but this time on a completely new basis: the relationship between God and creation now rests on an agreement in which God sets boundaries for himself alone. The 'recreation' that follows the flood does not include the restoration of unimpeded channels of communication between the divine and the human. God knows that the human response will be flawed and that wanton killing will not cease and therefore utters a statement that requires no human response. Regardless of human actions in the future, God promises never to destroy the earth again.

The legal component of the flood story also allowed the biblical authors to project Israel's unique, monotheistic outlook. Flood stories were a feature of several myths and epics of ancient Mesopotamia, and the biblical version may very well have had its source in those myths.[10] But the legal material balances the mythological elements by depicting God with an assertion of his otherness. As in Gen. 1.22, 28, the deity charges all living creatures with the responsibility of procreation but is himself separate from that process. Under the mandate, the monotheistic outlook prevails by balancing God's role as the source of all life with the insistence that although he controls sexuality and fertility, he is separate from them.[11] This theme is

10. See *The Epic of Gilgamesh* (trans. M.G. Kovacs; Stanford: Stanford University Press, 1985), pp. 97-103 (tablet XI), and *Atra-Hasis: The Babylonian Story of the Flood* (ed. W.G. Lambert and A.R. Millard) with *The Sumerian Flood Story* (ed. M. Civil; Oxford: Clarendon Press, 1969). For further reading see Damrosch *Narrative Covenant*, chapter 3, 'Gilgamesh and Genesis'.

11. See Cohen, *Be Fertile*, p. 14. This emphasis on fertility and procreation marks another divergence from the Babylonian flood stories. Indeed, according to the *Atra-Hasis*, the god Enlil sent the flood as a method

developed further in the prohibition of murder (4.5, 6) which asserts God's intimate connection to life in a manner unrelated to sexuality. Finally, the covenant which concludes the biblical flood story sets up a contract between God and the cosmos. God's mere anger or displeasure can no longer lead to so drastic a consequence as the total elimination of life. Even God, as it were, must yield to the rule of law, the law constituted by his own action.

Like the second account of creation, the Noah narrative has a sexual component which underlines the flawed nature of this liminal moment. The story of the reconstituting of life after the flood concludes with Noah planting a vineyard. He gets drunk and falls asleep in his tent in such a way that his genitals become exposed. Noah's son, Ham, comes upon him in this unseemly state and tells his two brothers, who then enter the tent without facing their father and tactfully cover him. When Noah discovers what Ham has done, he curses him, prophesying that he will be the slave of his brothers (9.20-28). This tale is a startling and unsettling conclusion to the account of God's renewal of his relationship with humanity: the charge of פרו ורבו in the post-flood narrative is not followed by an account of Noah having sexual relations with his wife and thus continuing the line begun with Adam.[12] Instead, the Bible presents an account of exposure with incestuous and even homosexual

---

of population control and had no thought of future repopulation of the earth: all humanity would have been annihilated if the god Enki had not interceded. See B.R. Foster, *Before the Muses: An Anthology of Akkadian Literature* (Bethesda, MD: CDL Press, 1993), I, pp. 182-83, and A.D. Kilmer, 'The Mesopotamian Concept of Overpopulation and its Solution as Reflected in the Mythology', *Or* 41 (1972), pp. 160-77. I wish to thank W.W. Hallo for this insight.

12. H.H. Cohen proposes that Noah planted the vineyard and drank the wine it produced precisely in order to enhance his procreative abilities, citing other accounts in the Bible where intoxication from wine precedes sexual activity (or intended sexual activity)—as in the case of Lot (Gen. 19.31-36) and Uriah the Hittite (2 Sam. 11.13). He also notes that wine and sexuality are commonly associated in the ancient pagan world. (*The Drunkenness of Noah* [University, Alabama: University of Alabama Press, 1974], chapter 1.) Cohen's reading makes Noah's failure all the more poignant.

overtones which seems to undercut the divine's renewed affirmation of life.[13]

The appellation of Noah here as איש האדמה ('man of the soil') (9.20) further calls into question the covenant between God and humanity by alluding to Cain, the עבד אדמה ('tiller of the soil', 4.2) whose offering of the 'fruit of the soil' was displeasing to God and who subsequently murdered his brother. Even Noah, who was deemed by God the only human worthy of not being destroyed, emerges in the end as painfully fallible. Utnapishtim, the lone survivor of the flood in the Babylonian flood story, *Atra-Hasis*, is deified after the flood. Noah, however, remains mortal and thus flawed. In the biblical flood story, therefore, law and narrative interact to undercut the promise of the post-diluvian narrative and to foreclose any idealized or mythologized view of history.

Paradoxically, it is this very flawed nature of the biblical subject which is valorized within the biblical worldview. Humanity in the Bible is defined by its fallibility. Those moments in biblical narrative history when humanity seems most elevated are also, therefore, the moments when it is most deflated: monotheism, as the dialogic tension between the divine and the human, replaces the mystifications of polytheism with the imperfections of a polyphonic universe.

13. Cohen finds that by gazing upon his father's genitals, Ham is actually attempting to usurp his father's generative capacity (*Drunkenness*, pp. 14-16). This reading, though it differs from mine, also highlights the flawed nature of this moment of regeneration after the flood.

Chapter 4

SINAI: LAW AND LANDSCAPE

Although the narrative concerning the revelation at Sinai depicts the liminal moment that forms the basis of all biblical narrative history, it too remains incomplete and unfulfilled. The themes of alienation and conflict that have dominated previous liminal moments are present here as well, reinscribed in the aural and visual image schemes of voice (far–near) and topography (up–down).[1] The narrative falls into two parts. In the first part (Exod. 20.1-15), the Israelites are privileged to hear God's voice as he enters into a covenant with them; in the second part (Exod. 32), this intimacy is undermined with the account of the apostasy involving the golden calf. The conflicting themes of intimacy and alienation also co-exist within each part: while the first emphasizes God's closeness to Israel, the narrative also stresses his separateness; conversely, while the second focuses on God's anger and destructive powers, it also highlights his ongoing involvement with Israel.

Law plays a major role in encapsulating this thematic polyphony in both segments of this most important of moments. In addition to the Decalogue that looms so large in the first part, there are also laws concerning the prohibition of idolatry and the building of an altar (20.19-23).[2] In the second part the Decalogue is not present, but laws forbidding idolatry and concerning the establishment of the cult are expanded (34.10-26). What is central in the first is secondary in the other, and vice versa. The legal material in each section merges different issues that both interact with and modify each other, yet neither

1. See G. Lakoff, *Women, Fire, and Dangerous Things: What Categories Reveal about the Mind* (Chicago: University of Chicago Press, 1987).
2. Some Bible versions number these verses as 20.22-26.

harmonizes them nor diffuses their dialogic tension. All of the laws, however, are concerned with the primary theme of the narrative: the unique and problematic nature of God's relationship with Israel.

God's desire for intimacy with Israel is the primary theme of the first section of the Sinai narrative, yet the text repeatedly emphasizes the potentially life-threatening aspect of God's proximity as well. Thus in Exod. 19.4-5, God describes the bonds that tie the Israelites to him: 'You have seen what I did to the Egyptians, how I bore you on eagles' wings and brought you to Me'. Further he speaks of Israel as being 'my treasured possession (סגלה) among all the peoples', and continues with an account of the heights to which the Israelites will be raised: 'But you shall be to Me a kingdom of priests and a holy nation' (19.6). Yet at the same time, the people are constantly admonished to keep their distance on pain of death, a warning repeated no less than three times in ch. 19 (vv. 12-13, 21, 24).[3] Only Moses can withstand God's overwhelming presence; his role as mediator between God and the people is emphasized throughout this chapter. Operating topographically along a vertical axis, and aurally as the conduit between the voice of God and the voices of the people, Moses repeatedly goes up and down the mountain delivering messages; he is polyphony incarnate. Thus the preamble to the account of the revelation, the beginning of ch. 19, constructs a very mixed and even contradictory image/picture: God has brought the Israelites to his bosom, but this intimacy is terrifying and fraught with danger. Such a situation cannot be sustained for long in unmediated form.

---

3.   In his book *God's Phallus and Other Problems for Man in Monotheism* (Boston: Beacon Press, 1994), H. Eilberg-Schwartz also discusses the threatening, even devastating consequences to humans of the immediacy of the divine presence:

> The Israelite religion imagines contact with the deity as a terrifying experience. The incursion of the sacred into the realm of the profane is devastating and results in death and disorder. This explains why boundaries have to be set around the mountain for God's appearance, why God hides in a cloud, is protected in a Temple behind veils, and why God only lets Moses see the divine back (p. 151).

On the third day, the nation is confronted with lightning, thunder and the sound of rams' horns, all of which serve as a prologue (19.16-19) to the sound of God's direct, unmediated voice uttering the Decalogue, his first legal pronouncement to his newly redeemed people. This juxtaposition of divine display and divine message serves to illuminate still further the dual nature—combining closeness and unbridgeable distance—of God's relationship with Israel. God speaks, but it is not at all clear that he is heard. The awesomeness of the display of the divine presence seems to blot out the content of his speech. Both aural and visual communication are profoundly disrupted as the people are overwhelmed by the primal power manifested in the sights and sounds that engulf them:

> All the people witnessed the thunder and lightning, the blare of the horn and the mountain smoking; and when the people saw it, they fell back and stood at a distance (20.15).

This loss of bearing on the part of the nation is highlighted by the blurring of the senses indicated in the synesthesia of seeing and hearing: וכל־העם ראים את־הקולת ואת־הלפידם ואת קול השפר ואת־ההר עשן ('All the people saw the thunder and lightning, the blare of the horn and the mountain smoking'). The dinning repetition of ואת in this verse adds to the feeling of total bombardment.

The people cannot withstand this manifestation of God's power; the very awesomeness of the delivery, ironically, makes a response virtually impossible. Rather than respond, the people again ask Moses to act as their mediator: 'You speak to us, they said to Moses, and we will obey; but let not God speak to us, lest we die' (20.16). From then on God withdraws from direct communication with the Israelites and Moses resumes his role as human agent, both addresser and addressee of divine legal pronouncements. The channels of communication between God and the people are thus unstable even at the moment of greatest closeness. Indeed, the very laws that constitute the Israelite community must be delivered through a mediator. Even as Moses fulfills this bridging function he illuminates the gap in communication, and the topography of the mountain, by imparting a spatial dimension, further emphasizes the immediacy and yet inaccessibility of divine speech communication.

The dual nature of God's relationship with Israel in this

narrative is of crucial importance from the point of view of biblical ideology. Nowhere else in the Bible, with the exception of the primeval history and certain moments in the patriarchal narratives, is God anthropomorphized to such a degree. The Ten Commandments function as the fulcrum in this delicate balancing act between closeness and distance. In terms of pure information, there is no real need for them to appear here: all of these laws appear elsewhere in the Bible in one form or another. However, in their concise presentation in the Decalogue, the laws are a distillation of the entire legal corpus of the Bible, and they emblematize—in their iconic inscription on the tablets—the importance of law in the relationship between God and Israel.[4] In terms of biblical ideology, then, law serves as the crucial mediating factor in the interaction between God and his people. It provides a means of communication but preserves the proper distance: law is a literal, textual embodiment of God, yet also a distancing—through mediated or inscribed speech—of humanity from any physical conception of God.

The tension present in the narrative as it attempts to maintain a vision of immanence and transcendence in the depiction of the divine is also evident in the Ten Commandments themselves. The first five deal with God's omnipotence and majesty and his special relationship with Israel. (While the fifth commandment— honor your father and mother—lacks this specific focus, it can be seen as a transition leading to the second half.) The emphasis on God's grandeur and majesty is reinforced by an allusion to the first version of creation in the commandment to observe the Sabbath (19.8-11).[5] In contrast, the second half deals with the necessary but mundane functioning of human society. These laws could appear in the statutes of any nation; they do not

---

4. Cassuto sees the Decalogue itself as a preamble to the covenant:

> Thus the Ten Words are not the substance of the covenant, nor its conditions, but the introduction to it. Before the particulars and terms of the covenant are conveyed by the intermediary, God Himself makes a prefatory declaration that establishes the basic principles on which the covenant will be founded (*Exodus*, p. 239).

5. This is the commandment in the Exodus Decalogue that differs most from the version in Deuteronomy (5.12-15), where observance of the Sabbath is linked to the exodus from Egypt rather than to the creation.

deal directly either with God's dominion over creation or his special relationship with Israel. Nevertheless, they play an important role by lessening the overwhelming impact of the divine immediacy that resonates in the first part of the Decalogue.

The commandments thus encapsulate the basic themes of the narrative much as the divine injunctions did in the two creation stories. In other words, the narrative tension between immediacy and distance is mirrored in the structure of the Decalogue. The two visions are never completely harmonized either in the narrative or in the laws—nor can they be from the point of view of monotheistic ideology. The biblical understanding of the monotheistic God lies precisely in maintaining the tension between the two, and one function of the Decalogue is to highlight that tension.

David Damrosch, in his book *The Narrative Covenant*, sheds further light on the interweaving of law and biblical narrative history in the account of the revelation at Sinai.[6] Damrosch finds that '[t]he singularity of the giving of the Law at Sinai is extended, through the rituals inaugurated at Sinai itself, to a narrative order of varied repetition'.[7] In this fashion, he observes, the ritual laws impart to the historical account of the theophany imperfective qualities and thus timeless resonance.[8] He does not focus, however, on the fact that the theophany *itself* takes the form of law. All biblical law is interwoven with narrative history, but perhaps nowhere do the two come together more markedly than in the theophany at Sinai, where they are presented in the biblical text as one and the same. Because of its interaction with law, history takes on qualities of continuation and repetition which look to the future; because of its association with history, law takes on the status of a

6. Damrosch limits his own study to ritual law and history in Leviticus, but his thesis can be broadened to include non-ritual law as well.

7. Damrosch, *Narrative Covenant*, p. 265.

8. There are two main tenses in biblical Hebrew, the perfect and the imperfect. The perfect tense describes actions that are already completed while the imperfect denotes actions or states that are not completed. Included in the imperfect are actions that will take place in the future, actions that are habitual or customary, and potential or probable actions.

hallowed and venerated monument in Israel's past. In combining the two, the biblical authors were able to endow the depiction of this most important of Israelite liminal moments with a depth and complexity that would not otherwise have been possible.

An Altar of Earth

Compared to the almost seamless blending of law and narrative in the account of the theophany, the instructions that follow concerning idolatry and the altar seem at first to be awkwardly tacked on, even out of place (20.19-23):

> The Lord said to Moses:
> Thus shall you say to the Israelites: You yourselves saw that I spoke to you from the very heavens: With Me, therefore, you shall not make any gods of silver, nor shall you make for yourselves any gods of gold.[9] Make for me an altar of earth and sacrifice on it your burnt offerings and your sacrifices of well-being, your sheep and your oxen; in every place where I cause My name to be mentioned I will come to you and bless you. And if you make for Me an altar of stones, do not build it of hewn stones; for by wielding your tool upon them you have profaned them. Do not ascend My altar by steps, that your nakedness may not be exposed upon it (20.19-23).

The appearance of these ritual laws at this point raises several questions. Is this seemingly self-contained legal/ritual textual unit to be read in relation to the 'Book of the Covenant' (the name scholars conventionally ascribe to the series of laws that begins ch. 21 and concludes with ch. 24)[10] that follows or to the Decalogue that precedes it? The situation is further complicated

---

9.   There are syntactic problems with the Hebrew of v. 23 which the English translation glosses over. The verse begins with the statement לא תעשון אתי ('You shall not make with Me') and concludes with לא תעשו לכם ('you shall not make unto you'), and it is not clear from the text whether the gods of silver and gods of gold are to be linked to the beginning of the verse or to the end. Since the problem is not central to my discussion, I will not attempt a reading. Nehama Leibowitz discusses the various rabbinic commentaries in *Studies in Shemot* (2 vols.; trans. A. Newman; Jerusalem: Word Zionist Organization, 1976), pp. 352-56.

10.   See Sarna *Exodus*, pp. 117-18

by the fact that the Decalogue already contains a prohibition against idolatry, and the instructions to Moses concerning the construction of the Tabernacle and the altar contain cultic regulations in great detail. What purpose, then, does the insertion of these brief regulations serve here?

For Everett Fox, this body of laws functions 'as an introduction to the general body of legislation that begins the next chapter. Like Israel's other law collections in Leviticus and Deuteronomy, it starts with rules pertaining to worship'.[11] Fox's explanation is not completely satisfactory, however, as he ignores the laws' context, their possible link to the preceding narrative of the theophany—a link suggested by the language of v. 19 that begins these regulations: 'You yourselves saw that I spoke to you from the very heavens'.

Another view is provided by Nahum M. Sarna, who finds that vv. 19-23

> bridge the foregoing and following sections. They continue the preceding narrative by featuring the instructions that Moses received as he 'approached the thick cloud'; they also serve as a crucial introduction to the following laws because without verse 19 (22) there would be no antecedents to 21.1.[12]

Although Sarna's reading attempts to link the three units, he does not discuss the connection of the regulations in vv. 20-23 to their context but focuses primarily on the prefatory statement in v. 19. Umberto Cassuto, like Fox, includes vv. 19-23 with the statutes and ordinances of the Book of the Covenant;[13] however, he also attempts to read them in light of the revelation narrative that comes earlier. In discussing v. 21 concerning the altar, Cassuto states:

---

11. E. Fox, *Now These are the Names: A New English Rendition of the Book of Exodus* (New York: Schocken Books, 1986), p. 117.

12. Sarna, *Exodus*, p. 115.

13. U. Cassuto, *A Commentary on the Book of Exodus* (trans. I. Abrahams; Jerusalem: Magness Press, 1967 [1951]), p. 254. Childs also includes the altar regulations with the Book of the Covenant (B.S. Childs, *The Book of Exodus: A Critical Theological Commentary* [Philadelphia: Westminster Press, 1974], p. 460).

As for the passage under discussion, we must not loose sight of
the fact that it belongs to the narrative following immediately
after the story of the Revelation at Mount Sinai, and is to be
understood only against that background.[14]

I, too, discern a link between the altar regulations and the
account of the theophany; however, where Cassuto's reading
centers on v. 21, I find the entire series of instructions to be
related to the account of the revelation at Sinai. I believe the
legal instructions have a crucial role to play in highlighting the
flawed nature of even this exalted moment. Setting forth ritual
laws concerning the altar at this point serves to undercut and
deflate the narrative of the revelation at Sinai and highlights the
tensions inherent in the account itself—as law usually does in
biblical moments. The regulations further elaborate on the linked
themes of intimacy and alienation and maintain intertextual
relations with the second part of the theophany narrative as
well. A close reading of vv. 19-23 demonstrates that these
regulations serve both to conclude the account of the first
revelation at Sinai and as a bridge, not so much to the Book of
the Covenant, as to the account of the apostasy of the golden
calf and the restoration of the covenant. Consider the injunction
against images of silver or gold:

> With me, therefore, you shall not make for yourselves any gods
> of silver, nor shall you make for yourselves any gods of gold
> (20.20).

This may seem at first to be a further of elaboration of the third
commandment:

> You shall not make for yourself a sculpted image, or any likeness
> of what is in the heavens, or on the earth below, or in the waters
> under the earth (20.4).

But there is a difference. While the prohibition in the Decalogue
relates to images of pagan gods, as Cassuto shows quite
convincingly, v. 20 forbids the worship of the God of Israel in
the manner of the surrounding polytheistic nations:

14. Cassuto, *Exodus*, p. 256.

This verse is not redundant even after the prohibition in the Decalogue. There the general principle is stated forbidding the making of any likeness, whereas here particular examples of the law are given. Even if the aim be to honor the God of Israel (*with Me*), and even if such precious metals as silver and gold be used, with which other nations do honour to their gods, you may not make any divine image. Even the most exquisite ornamentation cannot serve as a fitting symbol of the Invisible God.[15]

He then goes on to link v. 21 to the prohibition of ornamentation:

Even the worship in My honour should not resemble the ornate ritual of the gentiles, who build ornate altars to their gods, but should be very simple: *An altar of earth you shall make for Me...*[16]

Cassuto's reading is most insightful, yet it fails to note that ornamentation was not in fact eliminated from the cult; indeed, gold and silver form leitmotifs in the entire Sinai unit. They reappear in the divine instructions to Moses concerning the construction of the Tabernacle (25.3), in the apostasy of the golden calf (32.2), and again in the account of the actual building of the Tabernacle (35.5). In fact, the contrast between gold and silver, on the one hand, and earth, on the other goes beyond a mere prohibition of grandeur in the worship of God. These materials—silver, gold, and earth—also take on a metaphorical meaning, and it is this meaning the Bible uses to incorporate this flawed liminal moment into the Sinai narrative.

In a sense, opposition between precious metals and earth encapsulates the tensions inherent in the revelation narrative as a whole. The emphasis on earth, first of all, serves to diminish the Israelites at the moment when they have attained the greatest heights. It also echoes the associations between earth (אדמה) and human mutability found in other liminal moments: as with the narratives concerning Adam, Cain, and Noah, introducing אדמה serves to temper the mythopoeic potential of the account of the theophany. The ritual directive concerning an altar of earth, coming at the conclusion of the first part of the Sinai narrative, 'activates' the symbolic meaning earth acquired

---

15. Cassuto, *Exodus*, p. 255.
16. Cassuto, *Exodus*, p. 255.

at other liminal moments, and thereby brings in those meanings to illuminate the flawed nature of this liminal moment as well.[17]

In the particular context of the revelation at Sinai, however, earth takes on a more complex meaning than in other instances. Whereas in the accounts of Cain and Noah it functioned to deflate humanity by pointing up human failings, here earth is also a source of blessing. The altar regulations posit the ideal biblical vision of human–divine interaction. It is precisely when the Israelite approaches the deity from the framework of his mutability, symbolized by earth, that his offering is accepted and blessed, and the deity is most accessible. An offering presented from a humble, low altar of earth, whatever the type of offering or the kind of animal, allows a bridging of the distance between the human and the divine:

> Make for Me an altar of earth and sacrifice on it your burnt offerings and your sacrifices of well-being, your sheep and your oxen; in every place where I cause My name to be mentioned I will come to you and bless you (20.21).

The altar thus serves as a palpable symbol of both human fallibility and divine magnanimity, and as such embodies the theme of closeness/distance found in the theophany narrative as a whole. The text conveys the message that even though—or perhaps just because—the newly emacipated and covenanted Israelites have attained heights never achieved by any other nation, they are still human and therefore ephemeral; their cult must reflect the fact that they are, as it were, earthbound.

Gold and silver, on the other hand, are identified in the altar regulations with forbidden forms of worship. Cassuto quite rightly points out that the prohibition in v. 20 is concerned not so much with paganism as with the improper worship of the God of Israel.[18] In this sense, gold and silver are associated with humanity forgetting about its mutability and reaching for a grandeur and glorification in a way that is tantamount to an act of defiance of God himself. Precious metals here fulfill the role filled by the tower of Babel in Genesis (11.1-9): in both cases,

---

17. See R. Alter's discussion of allusion in the Bible, in his book *The World of Biblical Literature* (New York: Basic Books, 1992), chapter 5.

18. Cassuto, *Exodus*, p. 255.

crafts and artifice are linked metonymically and metaphorically to a humanity that oversteps its bounds in an attempt to overcome its mortality. Precious metals, in the context of the altar regulations, are the figurative expression for human self-aggrandizement and arrogance.

The biblical worldview finds something perverse in idolizing humanity and human achievement, so it is quite natural that the trappings of wealth and grandeur should be associated in these injunctions not only with forbidden forms of worship but also with forbidden expressions of sexuality. This relationship between theological and sexual transgression may help explain the concluding injunction against high altars, altars so high they would require stairs: 'Do not ascend My altar by steps, that your nakedness may not be exposed upon it' (20.23).

Paradoxically, from the perspective of the altar regulations, normative sexuality is good precisely because it is flawed, because it is associated with earth and thus human mutability. Perverse sexuality, on the other hand, is a sexuality that involves pleasure without procreation: the Bible finds repugnant the voyeuristic estheticization of sex, symbolically associated here with image-making and with the grandeur of high altars. The prohibition of nudity in the cult may allude to ancient polytheistic practices where pagan priests officiated in the nude. As Sarna states, 'ritual nudity is a phenomenon known to many religions. It is symbolically associated with both death and rebirth, and it also has a variety of magical uses'.[19] The Bible turns this pagan tendency towards self-veneration (and perhaps belief in self-regeneration) on its head by associating the exposure of the genitals with an empty grandeur that is meaningless precisely because it is divorced from life and procreation.[20] Instead, it stipulates a low altar of earth, associated with human vulnerability and mortality, as the appropriate place for Israelite worship.

The association of gold with image-making and improper sexuality also links these post-theophany instructions with the account of the apostasy of the golden calf (32.1-6). The

19. Sarna, *Exodus*, p. 117.
20. See Schneidau's discussion of the Egyptian god, Min, and the pagan belief in self-regeneration (*Sacred Discontent*, pp. 239-40).

connection is apparent not only in the reference to gold. The golden calf episode, set within the framework of the Sinai narrative, repeats the pattern of other liminal moments in which intimacy between the deity and humanity is sundered by human weakness and fecklessness. The altar regulations which immediately follow the account of the theophany function proleptically, hinting at this future downfall. With the announcement of these regulations, the betrayal of the covenant already resonates in the account of its inception, thereby casting an ominous shadow on the chances of its success.

Echoes of previous failures in the divine–human relationship also reverberate in the prohibition against using hewn stone in the construction of the altar: 'And if you make for Me an altar of stones, do not build it of hewn stones; for by wielding your tool (חרבך) upon them you have profaned them' (20.22). Although this is not directly stated, it seems clear that the prohibition associates the implement used to cut stone with the spilling of blood. This link emerges from the text's odd and unique use of the word חרב ('sword') for tool or implement.

Most translators render the Hebrew חרבך here as 'tool' or 'iron tool'; however, elsewhere in the Bible, the word clearly denotes a sword (Judg. 9.54; 1 Sam. 31.4; Ps. 45.4, etc.). BDB suggests the translation 'tool' in only a handful of cases, including Exod. 20.22, and only in the present passage is there no patent connection with violence. Although instructions for the building of the altar on Mount Ebal (Deut. 27.5; Josh. 8.31) specifically prohibit the use of iron, they do not refer to any particular implement. The use of 'sword' in the post-theophany instructions, therefore, is noteworthy, and would seem to indicate the authors' express desire to suggest a close association of hewn stone with violence and death. This juxtaposition of violence with the covenant at Sinai is not out of keeping with the theme of potential danger that runs through the entire unit. It augments the undertone of doubt and reservation regarding the covenant expressed in the prohibition against idolatry which begins this series, and further undermines the chances of the covenant's success.

Thus these very brief and concise regulations which seem to deal with straightforward ritual matters work on both a textural and a structural level to cast an ambivalent light on the theophany at Sinai and to deflate its central theme of Israel's elevation and uniqueness: instead of the heights of the mountaintop, the regulations stress the low and humble earth. The prohibition on uncovering of genitals links the altar regulations to the second creation story and to Noah, which depicted humanity at its most vulnerable and fallible. The metaphoric reference to killing in connection with hewn stone echoes the prohibition against wanton killing found in the post-flood legal instructions, and revives the focus on humanity's capacity for violence and destructiveness. Finally, the prohibition against gold and silver images foreshadows Israel's breach of faith with the covenant itself.

Whether these regulations conform to actual praxis is open to question.[21] However, the placement of this legal material at the conclusion of the Sinai narrative gives it significance far beyond the literal meaning of the laws themselves. By contrasting ornate fabrications with natural materials, and by reintroducing the theme of exposure of genitals, the instructions associate the account of the theophany with other moments that failed to live up to their promise, and in so doing intimate the unraveling of its promise as well.

The Golden Calf

With the story of apostasy of the golden calf, law becomes literally the embodiment of the failed communication between God and Israel. The divinely crafted tablets, carrying the inscription of God's publicly uttered laws, are shattered, and with them the concrete emblem of the direct link between the divine and human realms is irrevocably broken. Although Moses refashions the tablets (34.1, 27-28), the Decalogue itself is not verbally repeated in the text, nor does God again attempt to speak directly to the people. Indeed, what stands out in the account of the reinstatement of the covenant between God and Israel in ch. 34 is the absence of law, or more precisely, the

---

21. Sarna (*Exodus*, p. 116) discusses the available literary and archaeological evidence concerning the historicity of these injunctions.

absence of law as direct communication. Where one might expect a repetition of the divine recitation of the Decalogue, and thus a sense that the rift between God and Israel had indeed been truly healed, there is instead a poetic interpolation made by either God or Moses—the text is unclear—concerned with God's merciful and punitive attributes:

> The Lord passed before him and proclaimed: 'The Lord! the Lord! a God compassionate and gracious, slow to anger, and abounding in kindness and faithfulness, extending kindness to the thousandth generation, forgiving iniquity, transgression and sin; yet He does not remit all punishment, but visits the iniquity of fathers upon children and children's children, upon the third and fourth generations' (34.6, 7).[22]

After the golden calf, Israel is no longer privy to God's direct communication, and the second account of the theophany at Sinai is characterized by the absence of law as divine speech. This represents not only God's withdrawal from communication with Israel, but also the Israelites' inability to receive unmediated divine communication. In place of law as God's communicative act, the theophany that accompanies the reinstatement of the covenant assumes a generic form, that of poetry. The Decalogue is omitted from the renewed covenant ceremony because the link between God and Israel has not yet been repaired. Cassuto says of the reinstatement of the covenant:

> The ceremony was to be similar to the first one, but not so festive, just as the second wedding of one who remarries his divorced wife is not quite the same as the first. The breach has been healed but it is not possible to undo the fact that at some time the breach had existed.[23]

But this is not merely a matter of lack of ceremony. Implicit in the exclusion of the Decalogue from this second account of the

---

22. It is difficult to determine who is the subject of the verbs יתיצב and יקרא in v. 5, and thus who is speaking in vv. 6 and 7. Sarna finds that God makes the proclamation concerning his own attributes. Childs finds that 'Yahweh is most naturally the subject of the proclamation', but does not make clear who he thinks is speaking. See Sarna, *Exodus*, p. 215, and Childs, *Exodus*, p. 603.

23. Cassuto, *Exodus*, p. 438.

revelation at Sinai is the acknowledgment that what has been lost cannot be recovered. Instead, a totally different genre—poetry—substitutes for law at the moment of divine revelation. Law in this instance undermines the account by virtue of its very absence as a divine act of communication.[24]

The absence of the Decalogue represents divine withdrawal, but communication between God and Israel does not come to an end—this is not the complete cessation of interaction seen in the account of the tower of Babel—and law reappears at the conclusion of the account of the restoration of the covenant, albeit on a more distant and removed basis. Even if poetic utterance replaces the divine speech, legal communication does resume. As Everett Fox points out: 'God does not seem to agree to "go in their midst", nor does he give in and reinstate Israel with the term "my people"' (see 34.10).[25] God agrees to renew the covenant with the Israelites but he does not again refer to his special affection for them.[26]

24. B.S. Childs reviews the critical literature concerning the absence of the Decalogue in ch. 34 and proposes that ch. 34 is the J text's account of the Sinai covenant: 'A close look at the contents of the chapter confirms the thesis that an original covenant is being discussed. The theme of covenant renewal, which is confined to vv. 1, 4, 28b, is redactional' (*Exodus*, p. 607). But the crucial point surely is that the various strands woven together in ch. 34, regardless of their origin, offer in their present form a deliberate reiteration and renewal of the covenant, and this account of the renewal is meant to be read intertextually against the background of earlier covenantal narratives: the violated covenant at Sinai (ch. 32) and the post-diluvian covenant (Gen. 9). The absence of the Decalogue is thus textually meaningful, and in a larger sense part of the ongoing biblical dialectic concerning the relationship of the divine with his creation.

25. Fox, *Now These are the Names*, p. 193.

26. God's love for Israel and his forgiveness of their sins is of course a primary theme in the prophetic books. One such expression that relates particularly to the period of the wandering in the desert is the well-known passage in Jeremiah:

> I accounted to your favor
> The devotion of your youth,
> Your love as a bride—
> How you followed Me in the wilderness
> In a land not sown (2.2).

Omission of the divine utterance of the Decalogue from the account of restoring the covenant again points to the flawed nature of the people with whom the covenant is made, but God does not cease trying to enter into a dialogue with this difficult and recalcitrant nation, and thus the text turns again to legal discourse. The laws that accompany the account of the renewal of the covenant reflect the tension between the two conflicting biblical visions regarding the divine relationship with Israel; as we shall see, they embody both jeopardy and promise.

Forbidden Forms of Worship

The laws of the renewed covenant are divided into two series: the first (34.11-17) deals with the prohibition of idolatry; the second (34.18-26) with the annual cycle of Israelite festivals. According to Sarna, both series are attached to the renewal of the covenant because they 'concentrate on two fundamental issues that flow directly from the apostasy: inauthentic modes of worship (vv. 10-17) and the legitimate festivals and ritual obligations to God' (vv. 18-26)'.[27] These issues were, in fact, also the focus of the series of laws that concluded the first revelation at Sinai (20.20-23). However, the ambivalence suggested by those laws gains much greater prominence in the context of the aftermath of the apostasy. The prohibition of idolatry in this second version (34.11-17), following as it does on the heels of the apostasy, and quite clearly offering a response to it in its detailed description of the forms of forbidden worship, seems actually to foretell a future when these very prohibited activities will occur.[28]

Where idolatry was only obliquely associated with forbidden sexuality in the account of the first revelation, the two are graphically and intimately linked in the second, which further undercuts the restored covenant. Here, the text creates a chain

The Pentateuch, however, does not refer to Israel with such intimate terms as 'my people' in the passage concerning the renewal of the covenant—where one might have expected to find it—or in later passages.

27. Sarna, *Exodus*, p. 217.

28. The account of the apostasy at Shittim (Num. 25) describes just such an event, where improper sexuality and idolatry are linked.

of events framed by the expression זנו and והזנו ('play the harlot' or 'whoring'):

> Lest you cut a covenant with the settled-folk of the land: when they go whoring (זנו) after their gods and slaughter-offer to their gods, they will call to you to eat of their slaughter-offering; should you take their women (in marriage) for your sons, their women will go whoring after their gods, and they will cause your sons to go whoring (והזנו) after their gods (34.15-16).[29]

In its linking of perverse sexuality and idolatry, this prohibition differs markedly from the one in the Book of the Covenant (23.23-24), where the injunction is associated with fertility and blessing.[30]

> You shall not bow down to their gods in worship or follow their practices, but shall tear them down and smash their pillars to bits. You shall serve the Lord your God, and he will bless your bread and your water. And I will remove sickness from your midst. No woman in your land shall miscarry or be barren. I will let you enjoy the full count of your days (23.24-26).

The focus of this injunction is not so much on idol worship as on the intimacy between God and Israel.[31] Its extraordinary vision

29. This is the translation of Everett Fox (*Now These are the Names*, p. 192), which renders the Hebrew זנו as 'whoring' and not 'lusting' as does the JPS translation. I find Fox's rendering closer to the sense of the Hebrew original.

30. The prohibition against intermarriage (Exod. 34.15-16) also differs from a similar injunction in Deut. 7. Although it forbids the Israelites from intermarrying with the nations of Canaan lest this lead to idolatry, there is no link to prostitution in the Deuteronomic prohibition.

31. Intimacy is also the focus of the injunction in Deuteronomy, where it also has sexual overtones: 'It is not because you are the most numerous of peoples that the Lord *desired* (חשק) you and chose you...[my translation]; but it was because the Lord loved you...' (Deut. 7.7-8). These injunctions, in the Book of the Covenant and Deuteronomy, thus envision a totally different relationship than the ruptured one of ch. 34. The vision of the relationship between God and Israel as a love/sexual relationship between a man and a woman is part of a metaphorical system, in Lakoff's sense. Within this system, proper, procreative sex is associated with Israel's intimacy with God while deviant sex is linked to Israel's betrayal of its special relationship with God. This metaphor is particularly prominent in the prophetic books.

of the ideal Israelite community stands in stark contrast to the shrill negativity of the prohibition in ch. 34, which depicts the Israelites in a state of near-disintegration.

Furthermore, the prohibition of idol worship precedes the festival laws in the account of the restoration of the covenant but the order is reversed in the Book of the Covenant where the injunction against idolatry is part of the 'grand finale' to the entire series, which envisions an Israelite nation settled in its land and at peace within and without. In the account of the restoration of the covenant, the laws against pagan worship have a completely different emphasis: these laws envision an enemy which is far from defeated, an enemy which consists not only of the surrounding nations but also of Israel's own inner spiritual weakness. Thus sexuality in the context of the prohibition in the Book of the Covenant refers to fertility and longevity, whereas in ch. 34 it is linked to decline and decadence.

Following the apostasy of the golden calf, God is again forced to resign himself to the fact that Israel will not become his hoped-for ideal holy community. This is clear in the concluding statement of the injunction: 'You shall not make molten gods for yourselves' (34.17).[32] Nevertheless, the covenant is renewed, and God's relationship with Israel is resumed in full cognizance of the flawed, sinful nature of the people. Significantly, this move is affirmed in the regulations concerning Israel's divinely ordained festivals (34.18-26). The vision of settlement on the land within expanded secure borders, linked in the Book of the Covenant to the prohibition of idolatry, is here associated with the pilgrimage festivals:

> I will drive out nations from your path and enlarge your territory; no one will covet your land when you go up to appear before the Lord your God three times a year (34.24).

In this reiteration, however, the text presents a diminished vision. The borders are neither as expansive nor as clear-cut as in the Book of the Covenant, where they are described as stretching from 'the Sea of Reeds to the Sea of Philistia, and from the wilderness to the Euphrates' (23.31), nor is God's

32. The golden calf is referred to in 32.4 as a 'molten calf'.

bounty and beneficence depicted in the same detail. Nevertheless, the repetition of the festival laws in ch. 34 represents God's renewal of communication with his people and transmits a hopeful—if sobered—vision of the ongoing covenantal relationship.[33]

Moses: Veiled Communication

The ambivalence of the biblical approach to the restoration of the covenant is further developed in the concluding narrative. The Bible tells us that, unbeknownst to Moses, his face shone when he came down the mountain bearing the tablets of the law (34.29). Aaron and the people, seeing this 'afterglow of the refulgent splendor of the Divine Presence',[34] become frightened and retreat from Moses. It is only after he calls them back that they approach him and 'he instructs them concerning all that God had imparted to him on Mount Sinai' (34.32).

The text then switches from the depiction of a singular event—Moses' descent from the mountain—to the ongoing interaction between Moses and the Israelites. The divine radiance, apparently, remains with Moses, and he therefore veils his face whenever he speaks God's word to the people. The text, however, is unclear as to exactly when Moses uncovers (or covers) his face. The classical Jewish commentators, as well as Cassuto and Sarna, find that he uncovers his face when speaking as God's emissary but otherwise keeps it covered in public.[35] Childs, however, feels

33. The legal material in Num. 15, Dennis Olson notes, also inserts a conciliatory and hopeful note into the text, in that instance following the account of the colossal failure of Moses' spies to fulfill their mission (*The Death of the Old and the Birth of the New: The Framework of the Book of Numbers and the Pentateuch* [Chico, CA: Scholars Press, 1985], pp. 171-73).

34. Sarna, *Exodus*, p. 221.

35. Sarna, *Exodus*, p. 221; Cassuto, *Exodus*, p. 450. In her discussion of the meaning of this verse, Leibowitz (*Studies in Shemot*, II, pp. 638-40) cites commentators who understand it as stating that Moses spoke God's law to the people with his face uncovered. One commentator who does not read the text this way is Aaron Abu Alrabi b. R. Gershon (Ralbag). As Leibowitz recounts, he argues that:

the text is unclear on this matter,[36] and I agree. I would propose a reading which posits that Moses' face was always veiled when he was not in the actual presence of God, and in those moments when he serves as mediator to Israel.[37] Such a reading is in harmony with the themes of ambivalence, of closeness and distance, which begin the account of the theophany at Sinai and permeate the entire unit. The mediator himself is mediated by the veil: even Moses' own face becomes unendurable to the people.

The closing narrative, concerning the fear evoked in the Israelites by the radiance of Moses' face, thus highlights again

> Moses had to tone down, as it were, the spirituality of his message which they were now unable to cope with in its pristine form on account of their sin. This process of adjustment or dilution is represented in the placing of a veil on his face (p. 639).

Leibowitz does not agree with this reading. However, the Ralbag's interpretation fits in very well with the biblical depiction of God's renewed communication with Israel. The 'spiritual message' to which the Ralbag refers is after all *law*, law the Israelites are now unable to receive directly even from Moses. Moses as the surrogate deliverer of divine speech now assumes some of the attributes of the source and thereby becomes a second focus of the ambivalent relationship between God and Israel.

36. Childs, *Exodus*, p. 619.

37. H. Eilberg-Schwartz sees in the covering of Moses' face an aspect of his feminization vis-à-vis God: 'The veiling of Moses partially feminizes him. It points to his transformation into the intimate of God' (*God's Phallus*, p. 144). This view may be reinforced by the fact that the Hebrew verb קרן used in the text to depict the radiance of Moses' face, appears only one other time in the Bible, where it describes a bull with horns (Ps. 69.32). The root קרן in the Bible in fact almost always refers to horns, and Eilberg-Schwartz quite properly makes the association here as well. As he puts it

> The metaphor is clearly masculine; it calls to mind the prowess and might of bulls and rams, as well as an image of virility. At the very moment of Moses' feminization, then, a word is chosen that reasserts his masculinity . . . He is caught between genders—a man as a leader of Israel, a woman as the wife of God (*God's Phallus*, p. 145).

Eilberg-Schwartz has noted the metaphorical language most astutely. I find, however, that the covering of Moses' face symbolizes the continuing deterioration in the channels of communication between God and the people. After the apostasy of the golden calf, even Moses can no longer maintain entirely unmediated communication with the Israelites; the mediator himself thus becomes a degree further removed from the people.

the conflict between promise and jeopardy which is central to the Sinai narrative and to all other biblical liminal moments. The account of the revelation at Sinai began with a depiction of the divine presence, and of the terror-struck response to it, and concludes with the same theme.[38] Legal speech as an occasion for both closeness and distance thus frames the entire Sinai unit.

The radiance emanating from Moses' face, therefore, has several layers of meaning. Sarna finds that it represents 'the restoration of divine favor to Israel',[39] but my understanding of the text is not so unambiguous. The relationship of law and narrative in this section suggests that Moses' divine radiance may be read as an emblem of the very mixed biblical message concerning the resumption of God's relationship with Israel. Since the radiance marks Moses as the mediator of divine legal speech, he acquires some of the attributes of the addresser or originator of these acts. He too must be experienced, therefore, as separate from the people, and the interplay between closeness and distance that surrounded the original, revelatory speech act is now replicated in the mediated, modified one. By delivering God's message to the people, Moses is of necessity distancing himself from them. Thus this concluding segment of the Sinai narrative unit, the legal speech proceeding from an addresser through a mediator to an addressee, fails to achieve fully the rapprochment it was supposed to represent. Instead it results in a distancing, undermining its own communicative goals.

Even so, the law does signify the reinstatement of the covenant. After all, speaking and radiance are in fact linked in the text: light emanates from Moses' face as result of God's speech.[40] Indeed, the verb דבר (speak) occurs seven times[41] in

38. It seems fairly clear from the biblical text that when Moses 'instructs them concerning all that God had imparted to him on Mount Sinai' (34.32), he is in fact teaching law.

39. Sarna, *Exodus*, p. 221.

40. Leibowitz points to the three times that the radiance and speech are linked in the text (vv. 29, 34, 35) in connection with her discussion of the syntactic ambiguities in these verses, where it is not clear who is speaking to whom (*Studies in Shemot*, pp. 630-31). However, light and speech are linked whether God is addressing Moses or the reverse.

41. Cassuto and Fox note the sevenfold use of the verb דבר, 'speak', in

this concluding segment, and seems to function as a *leitwort* emphasizing the importance of the legal speech as the primary signal of God's readiness to renew communication with Israel.

The new tablets that Moses brings down from the mountain, paradoxically, also represent a more flexible and accessible communication. The first tablets, fashioned and written by God himself (32.16), were the embodied literal manifestation of the unmediated divine communication which the Israelites proved incapable of receiving. The second tablets are recorded by Moses from God's speech (34.28) so the focus shifts to law as abstract speech communication per se. The quality of the tablets as iconic, tangible representations of the divine presence is at some remove; they are still sacred, but not directly so. Law carved in stone is transformed into a physical object and can be shattered; it ceases to be vital and communicative. By contrast, law as communicative utterance becomes the locus of mediated revelation and thus partakes of human unpredictability and capriciousness. If the biblical generic conception of law is truly a functional rather than an essentialist one, then the legal text as physical object *must* be destroyed. From the point of view of biblical theology, the shattered tablets, while no longer bearing direct revelation, can speak in their very 'impurity' to the flawed humanity to which they are addressed.

The importance of Moses' role as mediator cannot be overstated. He serves as the means by which biblical law becomes embedded speech and thus accessible to human beings. Moses is critical to the entire biblical enterprise, for it is through his mediation that unfathomable divine law becomes communicative utterance. As Childs states with great sensitivity:

> Sinai is also the story of Moses, the mediator between God and Israel, who continued to function as a mortal man and yet who in his office bridged the gap between awesome, holy, and zealous God of Sinai and the fearful, sinful, and repentant people of the covenant.[42]

this textual unit (Cassuto, *Exodus*, p. 451; Fox, *Now These are the Names*, p. 195).

42. Childs, *Exodus*, p. 619.

Moses is thus the only human protagonist who is not undercut in the biblical depiction of a liminal moment. Unlike Noah, whose stature is diminished in the narrative that concludes the flood story, Moses has his status enhanced.[43] Although he is not—and from the biblical perspective cannot be—deified, his very physical being reflects divine splendor. However, his unmediated experience of God is not something he can share with others. The light radiating from Moses' face, which 'testifies to the restoration of divine favor to Israel', is too overwhelming for the nation to behold, and itself renders any act of direct communication impossible. Moses cannot transfer to the nation his own personal experience of God, but he can and does serve as mediator in transmitting law as the *linguistic* enactment of God's will.

43. Ultimately, Moses, too, is diminished: he is not permitted to enter the Promised Land (Deut. 3.23-28).

Chapter 5

LAW AND NARRATIVE HISTORY: JACOB AND HIS ASSAILANT

A Rite of Passage

The discussion of liminal moments thus far has progressed from primeval human history to a primarily national focus. I now wish to explore the role of law in a special liminal moment which serves as one of the primary transition points in the biblical depiction of the transformation of the Israelites from clan into God's elect nation. I refer to the episode in Genesis that recounts Jacob's struggle with the angel.

Jacob's family has just forded the Yabbok River; the biblical account proceeds:

> Jacob was left alone. And a man wrestled with him until the break of dawn. When he saw that he had not prevailed against him, he wrenched Jacob's hip socket, so that the socket of his hip was strained as he wrestled with him. Then he said, 'Let me go, for dawn is breaking'. But he answered, 'I will not let you go, unless you bless me'. Said the other, 'What is your name?' He replied, 'Jacob'. Said he, 'Your name shall no longer be Jacob, but Israel, for you have striven with beings divine and human, and have prevailed'. Jacob asked, 'Pray tell me your name'. But he said, 'You must not ask my name!'[1] And he took leave of him there. So Jacob named the place Peniel, meaning, 'I have seen the divine being face to face, yet my life has been preserved'. The sun rose upon him as he passed Penuel, limping on his hip. That is why the children of Israel to this day do not eat the thigh muscle that is on the socket of the hip, since Jacob's hip socket was wrenched at the thigh muscle. (32.25-33)

---

1. Fox renders למה זה תשאל לשמי as 'Now why do you ask after my name?', which is more faithful to the Hebrew original than the JPS translation (E. Fox, *In the Beginning: A New English Rendition of the Book of Genesis* [New York: Schocken Books, 1983], p. 134).

This is a liminal moment, obviously, because we are witnessing a transition from an individual patriarch to a national eponym. But the text itself is inscribed with other intriguing formations of liminality. One of these gives this episode a concrete, spatial dimension.[2] Sarna points to the fact the Yabbok river is 'mentioned in the bible exclusively as a frontier of Israel', and concludes that 'the assault upon Jacob is to frustrate his return to his homeland, to prevent him from crossing over into the future national territory of Israel'.[3] This episode deals with a border, or threshold, in the most literal sense. While the account of the revelation at Sinai has a vertical topographic orientation, pointing to the problems of communication between the domain of God and the domain of man, the topographic orientation here is horizontal. As space that must be traversed, the Yabbok provides a geographic inscription of liminality which, like Sinai, is threatening and forbidding. Fox notes the repeated use of 'crossing' in vv. 23 and 24, which 'clearly refers to more than just the river'.[4]

Roland Barthes, in his essay 'The Struggle with the Angel: Textual Analysis of Genesis 32.22-32', discerns three sequences in the episode—Crossing, Struggle, Namings—each dealing with change: 'What is in question in each is a *change*—of place, parental line, name, alimentary rite; all this keeping very close to an activity of language, a transgression of the rules of meaning'.[5] Barthes perceptively sees *transition* at the heart of the episode, both sequentially and structurally. What he finds interesting in the text is its

> abrasive frictions, the breaks, the discontinuities of readability, the juxtaposition of narrative entities which to some extent run free from an explicit logical articulation...the themes (Crossing,

2.   For analyses of this perplexing narrative see Sarna, *Genesis*; Speiser, *Genesis*; Fokkelman 'Genesis'. Another work of interest is Benno Jacob's commentary, *The First Book of the Bible: Genesis* (ed. and trans. E.I. Jacob and W. Jacob; New York: Ktav, 1974), pp. 223-25.

3.   N.M. Sarna, *Genesis* (The JPS Torah Commentary; Philadelphia: Jewish Publication Society, 1989), p. 403.

4.   Fox, *In the Beginning*, p. 135.

5.   R. Barthes, 'The Struggle with the Angel', in *Image, Music, Text* (trans. S. Heath; New York: Hill and Wang, 1977), p. 136.

Struggle, Namings, Alimentary Rite) are *combined* not 'developed'.[6]

At issue are the slippages, the ragged edges, the radical dislocations—all defining characteristics of liminality.[7]

Sarna gives particular prominence to the inherent instability in the account. As he points out, at the very moment when Jacob is about to enter the land and claim his birthright, an attempt is made to hinder, if not actually bar him from crossing over. The struggle threatens to physically prevent the liminal moment from taking place: inexplicably, God's messenger appears as a force of reaction, attempting to hold Jacob back and thus halt the inexorable forward movement of the divine plan for Israel.[8] It is as if, at the last minute, God has doubts about the relationship into which he is about to enter. Indeed, the episode at first appears to depict a negative response to Jacob's plea to God to affirm his promise to him (32.10-13). Only midway in the struggle does Jacob's sheer force of will tilt the balance in his favor.[9]

---

6.   Barthes, 'Struggle', p. 140.

7.   Recall P. Orecchioni's discussion of liminality, 'Dates-clés', referred to in Chapter 1.

8.   The episode concerning the attack on Moses as he returns to Egypt to take up his mission presents a similar account:

> At a night encampment on the way, the Lord encountered him and sought to kill him. So Zipporah took a flint and cut off her son's foreskin, and touched his legs with it saying, 'You are truly a bridegroom of blood to me!' And when he let him alone, she added, 'A bridegroom of blood because of the circumcision' (Exod. 4.24-26).

Here too, God, in seeking to kill Moses, inexplicably seems to be attempting to halt events that he himself had set in motion. A possible reading of this inscrutable episode is that, like the attack on Jacob, it presents a dissonant voice in the biblical polyphony, one that gives expression to doubt and ambivalence concerning the special relationship between God and Israel.

9.   Most commentators see this episode as foreshadowing Jacob's impending reunion with Esau; Sarna says the divine being is 'none other than the celestial patron of Esau-Edom, who is the inveterate enemy of the people of Israel' (*Genesis*, p. 404), thus echoing the Midrash Genesis Rabbah. Barthes sees the conflict with Esau as being 'displaced' onto the angel (God), who functions as the 'substitute of the elder brother once again beaten by the younger' ('Struggle', p. 134). However, although the

The ambiguity of this episode, its ideological instability and philosophical tension, are given particular emphasis and resonance through the legal addendum which concludes it. The law is framed as an etiological statement introduced by the formulaic על־כן: ...הנשה את־גיד בני־ישראל לא־יאכלו על־כן ('That is why the children of Israel to this day do not eat the thigh muscle that is on the socket of the hip, since Jacob's hip socket was wrenched at the thigh muscle', 32.33). It has the effect of binding the Israelite nation to the struggle of its eponymous forefather. The verse describes a dietary proscription in third-person narrative; the law is never presented as direct or even mediated speech. Rather than taking the 'normal' form of a prohibition or an injunction לא תאכלו, 'you shall not eat...', the prohibition is presented in terms of its effect on Israelite cultural practice: ...על־כן לא־יאכלו. Since we are given here the effect without the act, the legal intent seems deliberately vague. Significantly, this particular law does not appear as such in either of the two series of dietary injunctions (Leviticus 11 and Deut. 14.3-21) or elsewhere in the Bible.[10] This suggests that there might be aspects of the episode which the law memorializes but which biblical theology would rather keep at a distance, an element of taboo. It is not just the memory of the struggle per se that the law evokes; there is also an element in the encounter that future generations dare not replicate.

In fact, the story is replete with allusions to mixing or transgressing categories in a way not permitted in normative Israelite society. Not the least of these transgressions involve the story's homoerotic implications. Chana Kronfeld[11] notes this

episode certainly alludes to the coming encounter between the brothers, it seems also to be concerned at this moment of transition with the nature of the relationship between God and Jacob/Israel, and reflects the theological tensions inherent in that relationship.

10. Shunning the thigh muscle, with its link to Israel's eponymous father and thus to its very beginnings as a people, does function as a constitutive rule, i.e. a law by which a community defines itself (Searle, *Speech Acts*, pp. 50-53).

11. C. Kronfeld, 'On the Margins of Modernism', in *Contraversions: Critical Studies in Jewish Literature, Culture and Society* (Berkeley: University of California Press, 1996); see also Eilberg-Schwartz, *God's Phallus*, pp. 152-53.

aspect of the episode in discussing the poem 'Jacob and the Angel' by Yehuda Amichai.[12]

> Amichai's love encounter guides us to look anew at the biblical story of Jacob and the angel. We find in Genesis, through the prism of this poem, an intriguing erotic moment in the encounter between God and man, an encounter which, as we know, left Jacob-Israel injured in a very sensitive spot.

Amichai's poem makes explicit what is implicit in the Bible. And by making the encounter heterosexual, he sheds light on the latent homoerotic implications of the original biblical story.[13]

12. 'Jacob and the Angel':

> Just before dawn she sighed and held him
> that way, and defeated him.
> And he held her that way, and defeated her
> and both knew that a hold
> brings death.
> They agreed to do without names.
>
> But in the first light
> he saw her body
> which remained white in the places
> the swimsuit had covered, yesterday.
>
> Then Someone called her suddenly from above
> twice.
> The way you call a girl from playing
> in the yard.
> And he knew her name, and let her go.

(*Selected Poetry of Yehuda Amichai* [trans. C. Bloch and S. Mitchell; New York: Harper & Row, 1986], p. 40).

13. The verb used to describe the nature of the encounter between Jacob and the divine being, ויאבק, is unique to this episode, and its etymology is open to question. It is most commonly rendered as 'wrestling' (so Sarna, Fox, and Jacob). It may involve wordplay with both the names 'Jabbok' (יבק) and 'Jacob' (יעקב). Most intriguing, however, is one of the possibilities raised by Nachmanides (Moses ben Nahman, 1194-1270), who suggests that the letter א in the root אבק may actually have been a ח, and that therefore the verb originally was not ויאבק but ויחבק ('embrace'): 'Perhaps it is the way of the Hebrew language to interchange the *aleph* with the *het*' (Nachmanides, *Commentary on the Torah: Genesis* [trans. C.B. Chavel; New York: Shilo Publishing House, 1971], p. 405). He goes on, 'Perhaps this is the opinion of Onkelos who said, in translation of the word *vayeiʾaveik*, *veʾishtadeil*, and so also he translated the expression, "and if a man *yephateh*" (Exod. 22.15) "as if *yeshadeil*", if he embraces and kisses in the manner of

Jacob seems to transgress accepted monotheistic bounds in other aspects of the biblical account as well. Not only does he have physical contact with the divine being, he sees him 'face to face', bargains for a blessing, and then brazenly asks the angel for his name. S.H. Smith understands Jacob's request as an attempt to 'usurp the power of God himself'. I think this somewhat overstates the case but the request is nevertheless extraordinarily bold, and underscores the way this episode blurs the categories of divine and human.[14] In the biblical world-view such familiarity with the divine would ordinarily result in death[15]—Jacob notes the danger he had been in when he names the crossing at the Jabbok, Peniel (32.31). Yet at this epoch-making moment of transition and instability, he not only survives, but is even blessed.

Smith's view of this narrative and of the figure of Jacob in fact differs in numerous ways from the view presented here. Smith finds that Jacob emerges from his struggle and injury a chastened man, 'compelled to concede that his own procreative power is a blessing from God, not a free expression of his manly vigour'. He adds that

> by striking Jacob, symbolically, upon his genitals God demonstrates that only he has the power to bring Jacob's aspirations to fruition: what he has bestowed he can readily take away. Jacob must learn that lesson before his new role as Israel can properly take effect.[16]

Smith notes most perceptively the sexual overtones of the struggle, and its links to the battle between Jacob and Esau for the right to inherit the 'Abrahamic promise' of numerous

seduction' [transliterations are Chavel's]. Nahmanides thus suggests a possible homoerotic aspect to the encounter, relying on Onkelos, who in turn must have been relying on earlier traditions long since lost or suppressed. However, he retreats from such a daring notion—truly radical by traditional Jewish standards—and links the stem to the Hebrew word for dust אבק, the rendition with which his discussion began.

14. See S.H. Smith, '"Heel" and "Thigh": The Concept of Sexuality in the Jacob–Esau Narratives', *VT* 40.4 (1990), p. 464.

15. See, e.g., Judg. 6.22-23, 13.22, and Sarna's comment on the present passage (*Genesis*, p. 228).

16. Smith, '"Heel" and "Thigh"', pp. 472-73.

progeny. In fact, he finds—quite astutely—that the heel Jacob grabs onto at birth is a metonymy for Esau's genitals, 'the seat of procreation', as he puts it. Jacob thus symbolically attempts to appropriate for himself Esau's right to the blessing. But Smith fails to note the multi-layered nature of the account. The Jacob who appears in Smith's reading is a rather one-dimensional figure who evolves as a result of his struggle with the angel into a more worthy recipient of the divine blessing. The transition is much more messy than this, however, and it is precisely this lack of clarity which makes this episode such a paradigm liminal moment. Although Jacob's national significance undergoes pivotal change in this episode, the degree of his transformation *as a character* remains open to question. Nor is the issue of his right to the Abrahamic blessing completely resolved. To some degree Jacob wins by default; he simply refuses to yield. As is intimated in the account of the reunion between the two brothers, a shadow of a doubt remains about Jacob's legitimacy. The legal addendum, which highlights the national implications of the struggle by invoking a taboo that alludes to the maiming of Jacob's genitals, also hints at the problematic nature of Jacob's legitimate right to his father's blessing. This shadow of a doubt is transferred, through the dietary abstention, to his progeny as well.

The Thigh Muscle: Memory or Oblivion?

It is of crucial importance that Jacob is maimed in the place (כף הירך) which is metonymically the site of fertility and procreation—and of the Abrahamic covenant between God and Israel as embodied in the rite of circumcision.[17] The taboo regarding the consumption of the thigh muscle thus calls upon

---

17. Both S.H. Smith ('"Heel" and "Thigh"') and Stanley Gevirtz ('Of Patriarchs and Puns: Joseph at the Fountain, Jacob at the Ford', *HUCA* 46 [1975], pp. 50-54) find that, in the expression כף הירך, not only ירך ('thigh') but also כף ('hand' or 'palm') refer to the male sex organ. There seems to be a doubling of the metonymy, perhaps in the context of providing a balance with the expression גיד הנשה with which it is paired chiastically in the legal addendum: על־כן לא־יאכלו בני־ישראל את־גיד הנשה אשר על־כף הירך עד היום הזה כי נגע בכף־ירך יעקב בגיד הנשה.

the Israelites to identify with the great heights reached by their eponymous father while at the same time emphatically demonstrating that such an experience is not normative. The avoidance—through the dietary law—of the place of Jacob's injury, and the deflected castration that it may represent, serves as an ongoing reminder of their progenitor's immediate experience of the divine and of the life-threatening nature of that experience.[18] The taboo evokes both Jacob's elevation and his mutability—and, given the site of his injury, their own as well. In a larger sense, it serves to warn against the blurring of categories which, though an integral part of this one radically unstable liminal moment, is to be shunned. It thus tempers the mythopoeic potential of this enigmatic episode and serves as an ever-present warning: from the monotheistic perspective, the gap between the divine and the human cannot be bridged.

The legal postscript's focus on Jacob's injury further illuminates the multi-voicedness of this account. While the episode proper relates only that Jacob was struck in the hip socket (כַּף־יְרֵכוֹ) (32.26), the legal addendum adds a detail that is missing in the narrative: it specifies that the Israelites do not eat גִּיד הַנָּשֶׁה אֲשֶׁר עַל־כַּף הַיָּרֵךְ ('the thigh muscle on the socket of the hip') (32.33), since it was there that Jacob was injured.[19] Elsewhere in the Bible, יָרֵךְ appears as a metonymy for the male sex organ (Exod. 1.5; Judg. 8.30); the addition of the term גִּיד הַנָּשֶׁה in the legal addendum seems to intensify the focus on the genitals as the locus of Jacob's injury. Smith, basing his definition on the lexicon of Koehler and Baumgartner, says that it is

> the ischium at the base of the pelvis, and thus on the inner thigh.
> Perhaps the only real difference between *kp hyrk* and *gyd hnsh*,

18. Stephen A. Geller says of גִּיד הַנָּשֶׁה:

like that other sign of covenant, circumcision, [it] is a symbolic representation of the dialectic of positive and negative, blessing and curse. Like other cultic actions it stands on the dangerous frontier of holiness. ('Struggle at the Jabbok: The Uses of Enigma in a Biblical Narrative', *JNES* 14 [1982], p. 56).

19. The JPS Torah translates the גִּיד הַנָּשֶׁה as 'thigh muscle'; however, in fact its precise meaning remains unclear. Fox translates it as the 'sinew that is on the socket of the thigh', and Speiser refers to it as the 'sciatic muscle'. Sarna says of גִּיד הַנָּשֶׁה that 'venerable Jewish tradition identifies this unique and cryptic term...with the sciatic nerve'.

then, is one of specificity: the latter may be more directly
associated with the sexual organs in the region of *kp hyrk*.[20]

In my view, the additional detail imparts an extra dimension
to the law, one specifically concerned with future generations.
נשׁה derives from a root one of whose meanings relates to
forgetting, as in נשׁיה ('oblivion').[21] Given the strong lexical link
Hebrew establishes between masculinity and memory in the
root זכר—and the fact that in the Bible putting one's hand on
the male sex organ is a symbolic act in oath-taking[22]—the
insertion of the term נשׁה in the legal addendum brings in the
fuzzy line between memory and forgetfulness, and thus
underscores the blurring of categories, closeness and distance,
already found in the narrative itself.

Memory, and by extension history, thus seem to be called into
question in the dietary taboo whose very purpose is precisely to
evoke memory and whose etiological frame is meant to give it
historical resonance.[23] On the one hand, the law affirms that
Jacob's descendants did indeed become a nation among whose
founding memories is their progenitor's encounter with the
divine; on the other hand, the avoidance hints at partial
obliteration of that memory. The threat of annihilation which
hangs over the encounter—and which was seemingly overcome
with Jacob's transformation into Israel—reappears in the legal
addendum, casting a shadow over the destiny Jacob wrestled
so hard to secure. The addition of the term גיד הנשׁה as a more
focused euphemism for male genitals thus not only contributes
to the role of the law as a mechanism for both memorializing
Jacob's struggle and creating distance from it; it also hints at the
biblical ambivalence towards the relationship between God and
Israel that is being inaugurated with that very encounter.

20. Smith, '"Heel" and "Thigh"', p. 486. So also Gevirtz, 'Patriarchs',
p. 52.

21. For נשׁה as relating to forgetfulness see Gen. 41.51, Jer. 23.39,
Isa. 44.21 and other references in the concordance; note also the Arabic
cognate *nasiya* 'forget'.

22. See Gen. 24.9, 47.29.

23. See Meir Sternberg's brief discussion of etiology as 'temporal or
cultural bridging' (*The Poetics of Biblical Narrative: Ideological Literature and the
Drama of Reading* [Bloomington, IN: Indiana University Press, 1987], p. 121).

The law alerts us once more to the very murky dividing line in the biblical worldview between promise and jeopardy, between being maimed and being chosen, and between fertility and impotence.[24] In the Bible, liminality is fraught with uncertainty and danger and oblivion as well as with promise and blessing and continuity, and nowhere is this tension more evident than in the account of Jacob's encounter with the divine being which epitomizes Michael Fishbane's comment on the patriarchal narratives:

> What is so striking about these national religious memories of the original blessing and settlement is the awesome dialectic that exists between the precariousness of life, children, land, and food and the assuredness of the contrapuntal promise that YHWH is the master of Israel's historical destiny.[25]

The legal postscript succinctly brings together all of these elements and points to the very tenuous circumstances of this liminal moment, in which the divine and the human both intersect and clash with great force.[26]

The legal postscript to Jacob's struggle with the angel is thus a paradigmatic example of the role of biblical law as both a marker of auspicious beginnings and an agent of disruption and destabilization. The duality of voices in the postscript echoes and reinforces the polyphony present in the account itself. The account concludes with the emergence of a Jacob who, though wounded, has successfully passed his test. If the night is a symbol of danger and possible death,[27] the rising sun that

24. The theme of the initial barrenness of the matriarchs is also relevant here.

25. M. Fishbane, 'Composition and Structure in the Jacob Cycle', *JJS* 26.1-2 (1975), p. 37.

26. Barthes observes this volatility in his analysis of the narrative when he speaks of its 'abrasive frictions' and 'asyndetic character' ('Struggle', p. 141).

27. The crossing at the Yabbok has taken on a dual symbolic meaning in Jewish tradition. It is a place of life, but also a place of death. See Sylvie-Anne Goldberg, *Les deux rives du Yabbok*:

> c'est à son gué que jacob combat l'Ange et devient Israel (Gn. 32, 33), c'est de l'autre côté de celle-ci que tiennent les ennemis d'Israël (Nb. 21, 24; Jos. 12, 2)... Mais pour le Talmud (TB Hag., 13 b; TJ Hag., 2, 2 77d), elle évoque une rivière de feu, un purgatoire, qui délimite le lieu où se tiennent les morts

greets him as he crosses the river (32.32) celebrates his transformation into Israel, the eponymous father of God's chosen nation. This would seem to indicate that some resolution to the theological tensions inherent in the account of the struggle has been reached and that Jacob's blessing is now assured. Yet the legal addendum does not confirm that transformation; rather it reverses the process, and calls into question that which had seemingly been already promised.[28] Contradiction and opposition are thus present both in the relationship between the narrative of the struggle and its legal etiological conclusion, and in the internal tension exposed between the two conflicting visions of God's relationship with Israel.

Law as Etiological Tale

The encounter between Jacob and the divine being can be seen with considerable justice as the constitutive moment in the history of the covenant between God and Israel. Perhaps even more than the revelation at Sinai, the event marks the institution of this complex and often troubled relationship. It is an encounter of extraordinary physical intimacy between God and Jacob/Israel, one which involves both violence and eroticism. From the perspective of the patriarchal-monotheistic Israelite culture which produced this narrative, such an interaction would ordinarily be unthinkable. Metaphorically, of course, intimacy between God and Israel is not at all unusual: witness the repeated image of God the husband and Israel the wife. However, here the treatment is more literal than metaphoric—

dans le 'faisceau des vivants' (1 S 25, 29)—où sont réunies les âmes des Justes (*Les deux rives du Yabbok* [Paris: Cerf, 1969] [from book cover]).

One of the best-known works on Jewish Laws and customs of death and mourning is *Maavar Yabbok*, by Aaron Berachiah ben Moses of Modena (1626).

28. Robert Alter says of the account of the reunion between Jacob and Esau (33.1-17) that 'it has a look of disconfirming what has been so abundantly confirmed' (Alter, *World of Biblical Literature*, p. 207). As I see it, confirmation and simultaneous disconfirmation are already present in ch. 32, in the multi-voicedness of the legal postscript.

particularly in the specific concern with genitals—and has homoerotic overtones which diverge sharply from its usual heterosexual understanding. It seems that only an encounter of such force and intensity could cement the complex relationship between God and Israel while leaving its fissures so glaringly exposed and unresolved.

Evoking the dietary rule with this etiological tale rather than through direct speech communication allows the Israelites to place this overwhelming experience with the divine within an identifiable historical context while maintaining a safe distance from it. From the point of view of monotheistic theology, observing the law without a specific prohibition is almost a necessity in this particular case: observation of the law serves as an everlasting memorial to the reality of Jacob's struggle and its ramifications for subsequent generations of Israelites. At the same time, the omission of direct, divine, legal speech communication serves to counter-balance the awesome immanence of the divine presence in the narrative.

The etiological conclusion also highlights the central place that the struggle at the ford of the Yabbok holds in Israelite life and culture. Brevard S. Childs finds that etiological tales seek to explain present realities in terms of mythical causality: 'Central to this thinking is an understanding that a primeval act altered the structure of reality once and for all. The mythical element lies in the structural metamorphosis involved in the initial intervention'.[29] Childs goes on to suggest that 'in the genuine myth, an act performed by the eponymic father in the distant past altered the structure of reality and therefore it sought to do justice to this change'.[30] As Childs sees it, etiological tales are concerned with constitutive events in the history of a people, basic transformations that have ramifications for all generations to come. He distinguishes these 'genuine myths' from the non-mythical story in which 'an act in the past simply established a

29. B.S. Childs, 'The Etiological Tale Re-examined', *VT* 24.4 (1974), pp. 387-97 (390). For additional reading on etiology in the Bible see B.S. Childs, 'A Study of the Formula, "Until this Day"', *JBL* 82.3 (1963), pp. 279-92; and J.L. Seeligman, 'Aetiological Elements in Biblical Historiography', *Zion* 26.3-4 (1961), pp. 141-69 (Hebrew).

30. Childs, 'Etiological Tale', p. 393.

precedent which assumed an authority for later generations within a particular community'. As an example of such a *precedent-setting* as opposed to *constitutive*, etiological narrative, Childs cites the account in the book of Samuel in which David, after defeating the Amalekites, establishes the precedent that booty taken in battle is to be divided equally between the front and rear echelon troops (1 Sam. 30.24-25). In this account, he says, 'the change was one of custom; it involved no metamorphosis in the structure of the world or society'.[31]

By Childs's own definition, the account of the source of the prohibition on eating the sinew of the hip would be an etiology that 'alters the structure of reality'. Yet for some reason he does not assign it that role, but finds that 'this element has been subordinated within the final shape of the narrative to the main theme which focused on Jacob's change of name at Peniel'.[32] (Childs calls this a cultic etiology, but the dividing line between law and cult in the Bible is very hazy if it exists at all, as Childs himself has shown.[33]) In reading these closing passages as legal etiology, one sees that the preceding encounter indeed has an impact that is tantamount to altering the structure of reality. It is central to the Israelite community's self-definition and it contains the ambivalences, the multiplicity of voices, and the complexities of that community.

Indeed, the very noncanonical and 'imprecise' form of the law also points to the liminality of the event. As Chana Kronfeld has noted, the blurring of boundaries is the mark of liminal moments.[34] The fluidity of the moment in which the divine and the human realms intersect is also represented textually in the etiological conclusion: the quasi-narrative, quasi-legal aspect of the etiologic account interacts with the narrative proper to emphasize, through a mixing of genres or modes, the instability of the liminal moment. Significantly, this passage blurs the distinctions between the two genres most central to Israelite self-definition, law and narrative history.

David Damrosch has shown that the boundaries between law

31. Childs, 'Etiological Tale', p. 393.
32. Childs, 'Etiological Tale', p. 394.
33. See his 'Study in the Formula', pp. 287-88.
34. See Kronfeld, 'On the Margins of Modernism', Introduction.

and narrative history tend to blur even in the 'center' of the biblical enterprise, in the Priestly writings of Leviticus[35] and he notes 'the complex but harmonious interplay between two forms of narrative. Law and history meet on a common ground composed of ritual, symbolic, and prophetic elements'.[36] These basic characteristics of biblical poetics are already evident in the account of Jacob's transformation into Israel.[37] This is not to say, as James L. Kugel does, that in the Bible genre distinctions have no relevance.[38] To be sure, this culture evolved without a deep classificatory impulse, and generic categories do not have the meaning they would have, say, within a classical Aristotelian or neo-classical esthetic. Nevertheless, to the extent that law as a genre marks liminal moments in the Pentateuch, one can trace a functional view of genre within the biblical poetic. Law and narrative may intermingle, yet awareness of their generic differences still informs their rhetorical function; the fact that lines of demarcation become blurred does not mean they do not exist. As Searle points out: 'We could not recognize borderline cases of a concept as borderline cases if we did not grasp the concept to begin with'.[39]

The etiological addendum to the Jacob story presents a past projected into the future by means of a narrated present. Law is simultaneously narrative history and a call to future action. In this sequence the enactment of God's will and the communication that is God's text thus present, along the temporal axis, the same 'impurity' of voice and genre that is presented spatially in the revelation at Sinai

Bakhtin's view of genre as a fluid, functionally defined construct, which forces us to confront generic strategies in terms of their communicative and interpretive capacity is very useful in understanding the blurring of genre differences in the story of Jacob's encounter with the angel. Evelyn Cobley has

35. Damrosch, *Narrative Covenant*, p. 283.

36. Damrosch, *Narrative Covenant*, p. 263.

37. The account of Jacob's struggle with the angel is generally attributed to the J text. See Speiser, *Genesis*, pp. 255-57.

38. J.L. Kugel, *The Idea of Biblical Poetry: Parallelism and Its History* (New Haven, CT: Yale University Press, 1981), chapter 2.

39. Searle, *Speech Acts*, p. 8.

suggested that Bakhtin's theory of genre can best be characterized by his 'emphasis on difference or heterogeneity and his insistence on the ideological implications of genre'.[40] Bakhtin, Cobley continues,

> reminds us that literature is not just an aesthetically pleasing but also a culturally potent force. In his opinion, every literary text manifests a polyphonic diversity of disparate generic features which reproduces, in more or less displaced ways, the ideological struggles from which the text as such had been generated in the first place.[41]

The heterogeneric nature of the legal addendum, as both law and narrative history, thus reflects the multi-voiced complexity of the biblical vision inherent in the narrative account of the struggle. It both functions as a stabilizing, conservative force, emphasizing continuity and tradition, and at the same time points to the conflicted biblical vision of the event that it memorializes. Nowhere else in the Bible are the profound theological reservations concerning the relationship between God and Israel, on the one hand, and the intimacy and intensity of that relationship, on the other, conjoined more graphically than in this episode. The generically blurred structure of the legal addendum, functioning as both law and narrative history, provides an avenue to contain the volatility of these contradictory forces within the text, while still allowing dissonant voices to be heard. Unlike all of God's other attempts at connecting with his creation, as a result of this containment, this most ideologically freighted of biblical liminal moments ushers in a relationship between God and his elected nation which, though often tumultuous and difficult, will endure.

40. E. Cobley, 'Mikhail Bakhtin's Place in Genre Theory', *Genre* 21 (1988), p. 334.

41. Cobley, 'Genre Theory', p. 337.

Chapter 6

CONCLUSION: LAW AND MEMORY

With the legal etiologic account that concludes the account of
Jacob's struggle with the angel, law takes on a temporal
dimension: law becomes memory, instead of direct or even
mediated speech. Time and distance intervene between act and
response. In all other liminal moments discussed here, law
appears as present and direct speech—even at Sinai, where
Moses' mediation becomes necessary, there is still speech
directed at communicating with the Israelites. Yet in the Jacob
story, the legal practice is revealed by a physical act of the
community (observing the dietary prohibition) not a verbal act
of the deity or his emissary. With the etiological עַל־כֵּן, direct
speech has been replaced by a third-person narrative noting the
observance of the law. Memory and the axis of temporal
distance in this episode serve just as topography and the axis of
spatial distance did at Sinai. Space serves as the matrix for
negotiating distance in speech communication, but in textual
discourse only temporal sequence is meaningful.

What remains when speech becomes memory? What happens
when the Divine Word can no longer be heard and only the
record of that word remains? These are central questions of the
biblical enterprise.

Dennis Olson writes,

> This paradigmatic portrait of God wrestling with his people in
> every generation, always ensuring that his promises continue
> from generation to generation, characterizes...the structure of
> the entire Pentateuch.[1]

1. Olson, *Death of the Old*, p. 198. Indeed, Olson notes a concern with
continuity in the entire book of Numbers:

> The concern of the book is to establish a model or paradigm which will invite
> every generation to put itself in the place of the new generation with which

It is by reading and reinterpreting the narratives which inscribe their communal history that future generations of Israelites will be able to maintain the force of the legal dictates even without direct address. The biblical concept of memory pushes law away from pronouncement toward its end point, the stage of response. Thus Jacob's struggle with the angel, a narrative which metonymically launches the nation-building process, significantly ends with the establishment of law as the basis of communal memory.

But the primary example of the attempt to build group memory by means of law comes with the ritual laws concerning the commemoration of the redemption from Egypt (Exod. 12.1-36; 13.16). Throughout these passages, the laws focus on the present and the future simultaneously. Divine legal speech is aimed not only at those present, but at all future generations of Israelites. The full realization of these laws, then, involves not only the response of those present when God first uttered them but also the response of those not yet born.

How is obedience to these laws to be assured in the future? The Bible meets this challenge by constantly stressing the importance of memory as an essential element in the full performance of God's legal speech acts. Gabriel Josipovici states, 'the keeping of the Passover service, the observing of the statutes, has the simplest of aims: to keep memory alive'.[2] He fails to note that memory itself has the force of law in biblical theology: it too is the subject of a divine act. The account of the exodus is filled with allusions to memory as an integral element in the observance of the Passover laws. The root זכר ('remember') appears twice (12.14; 13.3), and שמר ('keep',

---

Numbers and the whole Pentateuch concludes... Many laws in Numbers are expressly given as perpetual statutes 'throughout your generations'. The flexibility and adaptability of God's laws as they encounter new questions and circumstances (Numbers 9, 15, 27, 36) provides a model for the ongoing interpretation of the traditions of the past for the sake of the present. The movable tent of meeting which reappears at the beginning of Numbers after the people leave the immovable mountain of Sinai (Num 1.1; cf. Lev 27.34) illustrates the need for both a fixed tradition (Mount Sinai) and a means by which to actualize the tradition as the people march through time (the mobile tent of meeting) (*Death of the Old*, pp. 183-84).

2.   Josipovici, *Book of God*, p. 137.

'observe') is repeated throughout (12.6, 17 (twice), 24, 25, 42 (twice) and 13.10).[3] Both roots are concerned with the intent of those to whom divine legal speech is addressed.[4] Sarna says that memory in the Bible

> connotes much more than the recall of things past. It means, rather, to be mindful, to pay heed, signifying a sharp focusing of attention upon someone or something. It embraces concern and involvement and is active not passive, so that it eventuates in action.[5]

Memory is crucial because it constitutes the basis of discourse, a discourse which in turn translates into action. Yosef Hayim Yerushalmi states: 'If there can be no return to Sinai, then what took place at Sinai must be borne along the conduits of memory to those who were not there that day'.[6] The conduits of memory receive expression in narrative, both oral and written.

In its harnessing of law and narrative, the exodus is unique in the Bible, for here law is presented as speech not only on the part of the divine but also on the part of those addressees, who are charged with keeping the force of the original acts through discourse and repetition:

> You shall observe this as an institution for all time, for you and for your descendants. And when you enter the land that the Lord will give to you, as He has promised you, you shall observe this rite. And when your children ask you, 'What do you mean by this rite?' you shall say, 'It is the passover sacrifice to the Lord, because He passed over the houses of the Israelites in Egypt when He smote the Egyptians, but saved our houses' (12.24-27).

The evocation of narrative history forces those fulfilling the laws of the exodus to focus—through memory or narrative

---

3. Cassuto discusses the repeated use of the root שמר in the account of the exodus (*Exodus*, p. 149); however, he does not include its occurrence in ch. 13 and therefore counts only seven instances.

4. Indeed, in its repetition of the Decalogue, the book of Deuteronomy replaces זכור—the verb used in the Decalogue in Exodus (20.8)—with שמור (Deut. 5.12) in the commandment to keep the Sabbath, demonstrating the semantic closeness of the two roots.

5. Sarna, *Exodus*, p. 13.

6. Y.H. Yerushalmi, *Zakhor: Jewish History and Jewish Memory* (Seattle: University of Washington Press, 1982), pp. 10-11.

reiteration—on the acts that engendered those laws: the response must harken to the past in order that it may continue to be performed in the future. As the distance from the giving of the law grows in both space and time, the responsibility for communication falls on the addressee, who must also now become addresser: it is incumbent on one generation to reiterate God's speech to the next generation.

This transition is oddly reminiscent of the primal acts of creation and the flood, where God was both addresser and addressee. But this is not the reflexive self-containment of the deity; rather the historical involvement and reinvolvement of the whole nation of Israel as the instrument of a historically concerned deity.

The critical importance of response to the laws concerning the exodus is illuminated by the textual emphasis. Three times we are told of the Israelites' absolute compliance with all of Moses' and Aaron's instructions (12.28, 35, 50), and two of these verses are nearly identical 'And the Israelites went and did so; just as the Lord had commanded Moses and Aaron, so they did' (12.28). Verse 50 intensifies the sense of total compliance by adding 'all the Israelites' to this statement. Where the first version of creation and the Noah story focus on divine lawgiving, in the exodus emphasis is placed on the response—a response that bridges the generations. Both vv. 28 and 50 follow instructions concerned primarily with Israelites not present at the exodus; in each case, the statement of satisfaction appears in the text after instructions clearly aimed at future generations of Israelites who will be living in the land of Canaan (v. 29 relates to the sacrifice of the Paschal lamb; v. 50 to circumcision). Nevertheless, the statement is set in the past, at the time the laws were issued.

The channels of communication between addresser and addressee are here presented as so open that the response takes place even though lawgiving has long since ceased. This becomes evident in the communication between different generations of Israelites depicted in the text:

> And you shall explain to your son on that day, 'it is because of what the Lord did for me when I went free from Egypt' (13.8).

And when in time to come, your son asks you saying, 'What does this mean?' you shall say to him, 'It was with a mighty hand that the Lord brought us out of Egypt, from the house of bondage' (13.14).

In these well-known passages—expounded upon in the Passover *Haggada*—performance of the Passover rituals engenders communication (typically in the form of question and answer) which in turn results in the continued performance of these laws. The close link between act and response is indicated in the narrative of the speaker, who recounts the events of the exodus as if he/she had actually witnessed them. Although the act is removed in time and distance, the response maintains the force of the act by means of ongoing discourse, both spoken and written.[7]

The focus on response in the account of the exodus highlights the underlying theme of this unit, the harmony present in the relationship between God and Israel at the moment of redemption. Nowhere else in the Bible except for the first creation story is the theme of harmony and inclusiveness so emphasized. In the account of the exodus, the multiplicity of biblical voices, often so dissonant, speak as one. Whereas law in other liminal moments often undermines or deflates the narrative in which it is embedded, in the exodus story it works together with the narrative to emphasize the momentous significance of the redemption from Egypt. Law and narrative are interwoven almost seamlessly here; as Fokkelman notes, they 'alternate and interpenetrate'.[8] In fact, they are so closely linked that law actually becomes narrative in the mouths of Israelites, who must perpetuate through speech and reiteration, the memory of the redemption from Egypt for future generations ('And you shall explain to your son on that day'). The need for Moses as the chosen human agent who acts as

---

7. Another example of law being pushed to its final stage is the quasi-autobiographical historical recitation that accompanies the offering of the first fruits (Deut. 25.1-9). Yerushalmi finds it to be 'a superlative example of the interplay of ritual and recital in the service of memory' (*Zakhor*, pp. 11-12).

8. Fokkelman, 'Exodus', p. 56.

both addresser and addressee is thus also eliminated. In the exodus passages, the Bible assigns this responsibility collectively to all generations of Israelites.

BIBLIOGRAPHY

Alter, R., *The Art of Biblical Narrative* (New York: Basic Books, 1981).
—*The Art of Biblical Poetry* (New York: Basic Books, 1985).
—*The World of Biblical Literature* (New York: Basic Books, 1992).
Amichai, Y., *Selected Poetry of Yehuda Amichai* (trans. C. Bloch and S. Mitchell; New York: Harper & Row, 1986).
Anderson, G., 'Celibacy or Consummation? Reflections on Early Jewish and Christian Interpretations of the Garden of Eden', *HTR* 82.2 (1989), pp. 121-48.
Bakhtin, M.M., *The Dialogic Imagination* (ed. M. Holquist; trans. C. Emerson and M. Holquist; Austin, TX: University of Texas, 1981).
—*Problems of Dostoevsky's Poetics* (ed. and trans. C. Emerson; Minneapolis, MN: University of Minnesota Press, 1984).
—*Speech Genres and Other Late Essays* (trans. V.M. McGee; ed. C. Emerson and M. Holquist; Austin, TX: University of Texas Press, 1986).
Bal, M., *Lethal Love: Feminist Readings of Biblical Love Stories* (Bloomington, IN: Indiana University Press, 1987).
Baltzer, K., *The Covenant Formulary in Old Testament, Jewish, and Early Christian Writings* (trans. D.E. Green; Philadelphia: Fortress Press, 1971).
Barthes, R., 'The Struggle with the Angel', in *Image, Music, Text* (trans. S. Heath; New York: Hill and Wang, 1977), pp. 125-41.
Bauer, D.M., and S.J. McKinstry (eds.), *Feminism, Bakhtin, and the Dialogic* (Albany, NY: State University of New York Press, 1991).
Biale, D., *Eros and the Jews: From Biblical Israel to Contemporary America* (New York: Basic Books, 1992).
Boyarin, D., *Intertextuality and the Reading of Midrash* (Bloomington, IN: Indiana University Press, 1990).
—'The Politics of Biblical Narratology: Reading the Bible like/as a Woman', *Diacritics* 20.4 (1990), pp. 31-42.
—*Carnal Israel: Reading Sex in Talmudic Culture* (Berkeley: University of California Press, 1993).
Carmichael, C.M., *Law and Narrative in the Bible: The Evidence of the Deuteronomic Laws and the Decalogue* (Ithaca, NY: Cornell University Press, 1985).
Cassuto, U., *A Commentary on the Book of Genesis*. I. *From Adam to Noah* (Jerusalem, Magnes Press, 1961).
—*A Commentary on the Book of Genesis*. II. *Noah to Abraham* (Jerusalem: Magnes Press, 1964).
—*A Commentary on the Book of Exodus* (trans. I. Abrahams; Jerusalem: Magnes Press, 1967 [1951]).

Childs, B.S., 'A Study in the Formula "Until this Day"', *JBL* 82.3 (1963), pp. 279-92.

—*The Book of Exodus: A Critical, Theological Commentary* (Philadelphia: Westminster Press, 1974).

—'The Etiological Tale Re-examined', *VT* 24.4 (1974), pp. 387-97.

Cobley, E., 'Mikhail Bakhtin's Place in Genre Theory', *Genre* 21 (1988), pp. 321-38.

Cohen, H.H., *The Drunkenness of Noah* (University, Alabama: University of Alabama Press, 1974).

Cohen, J., *Be Fertile and Increase, Fill the Earth and Master It: The Ancient and Medieval Career of a Biblical Text* (Ithaca, NY: Cornell University Press, 1989).

Cover, R.H., 'Nomos and Narrative', *Harvard Law Review* 97.4 (1983), pp. 19-25.

Damrosch, D., *The Narrative Covenant: Transformations of Genre in the Growth of Biblical Literature* (Ithaca, NY: Cornell University Press, 1987).

Dozeman, T.B., *God on the Mountain: A Study of Redaction, Theology and Canon in Exodus 19–24* (SBLMS; Atlanta, GA: Scholars Press, 1989).

Eilberg-Schwartz, H., *The Savage in Judaism; An Anthropology of Israelite Religion and Ancient Judaism* (Bloomington, IN: Indiana University Press, 1990).

—*God's Phallus and Other Problems for Man in Monotheism* (Boston: Beacon Press, 1994).

Finley, M.I., 'Myth, Memory and History', *History and Theory: Studies in the Philosophy of History* 4.3 (1965), pp. 281-302.

Fisch, H., *A Remembered Future: A Study in Literary Mythology* (Bloomington, IN: Indiana University Press, 1984).

—'Bakhtin's Misreadings of the Bible', *Hebrew University Studies in Literature and the Arts*, 16 (1988), pp. 130-49.

Fishbane, M., 'Composition and Structure in the Jacob Cycle', *JJS* 26.1-2 (1975), pp. 15-38.

Fokkelman, J.P., 'Genesis', in R. Alter and F. Kermode (eds.), *The Literary Guide to the Bible* (Cambridge, MA: Harvard University Press, 1987), pp. 36-55.

—'Exodus', in Alter and Kermode (eds.), *The Literary Guide to the Bible*, pp. 56-65.

Foster, B.R., *Before the Muses: An Anthology of Akkadian Literature* (Bethesda, MD: CDL Press, 1993).

Fox, E., *In the Beginning: A New English Rendition of the Book of Genesis* (New York: Schocken Books, 1983).

—*Now These are the Names: A New English Rendition of the Book of Exodus* (New York: Schocken Books, 1986).

Geller, S.A., 'Struggle at the Jabbok: The Uses of Enigma in a Biblical Narrative', *JNES* 14 (1982): 37-60.

Gevirtz, S., 'Of Patriarchs and Puns: Joseph at the Fountain, Jacob at the Ford', *HUCA* 46 (1975): 50-54.

Gumbrecht, H.-U., and U. Link-Heer (eds.), *Epochenschwellen und Epochenstrukturen im Diskurs der Literatur- und Sprachhistorie* (Frankfurt am Main: Suhrkamp, 1985).

Hartman, G.H., 'The Culture of Criticism', *PMLA* 99.3 (1984), pp. 371-97.

—'The Struggle for Text', in G.H. Hartman and S. Budick (eds.), *Midrash and Literature* (New Haven, CT: Yale University Press, 1986), pp. 3-18.

Hillers, D.R., *Covenant: The History of a Biblical Idea* (Baltimore, MD: Johns Hopkins University Press, 1969).

Jacob, B., *The First Book of the Bible: Genesis* (ed. and trans. E.I. Jacob and W. Jacob; New York: Ktav, 1974).

Josipovici, G., *The Book of God: A Response to the Bible* (New Haven, CT: Yale University Press, 1988).

Kilmer, A.D., 'The Mesopotamian Concept of Overpopulation and its Solution as Reflected in the Mythology', *Or* 41 (1972): 160-77.

Kronfeld, C., 'On the Margins of Modernism', in *Contraversions: Critical Studies in Jewish Literature, Culture, and Society* (Berkeley: University of California Press, 1996).

Kugel, J.L., *The Idea of Biblical Poetry: Parallelism and its History* (New Haven, CT: Yale University Press, 1981).

Lakoff, G., and M. Johnson, *Metaphors We Live By* (Chicago: University of Chicago Press, 1980).

Lakoff, G., and M. Turner, *More than Cool Reason: A Field of Poetic Metaphor* (Chicago: University of Chicago Press, 1989).

Lakoff, G., *Women, Fire and Dangerous Things: What Categories Reveal about the Mind* (Chicago: University of Chicago Press, 1987).

Leibowitz, N., *Studies in Shemot* (2 vols.; trans. A. Newman; Jerusalem: World Zionist Organization, 1976).

Milgrom, J., *Leviticus* (AB; Garden City, NY: Doubleday, 1992).

Moses Ben Nahman (Nachmanides), *Commentary on the Torah: Genesis* (trans. C.B. Chavel; New York: Shilo Publishing House, 1971).

Olson, D.T., *The Death of the Old and the Birth of the New: The Framework of the Book of Numbers and the Pentateuch* (Chico, CA: Scholars Press, 1985).

Orecchioni, P., 'Dates-clés et glissements chronologiques', in J. Dubois *et al.* (eds.), *Analyse de la périodisation littéraire* (Paris: Éditions Universitaires, 1972).

Pardes, I., 'Beyond Genesis 3', *Hebrew University Studies in Literature and the Arts* 17 (1989): 161-87.

—*Countertraditions in the Bible: A Feminist Approach* (Cambridge, MA: Harvard University Press, 1992).

Polzin, R., *Moses and the Deuteronomist; A Literary Study of the Deuteronomic History.* Part I. *Deuteronomy, Joshua, Judges* (New York: Seabury Press, 1980).

Reed, W.L., *Dialogues of the Word; The Bible as Literature according to Bakhtin* (New York: Oxford University Press, 1993).

Sarna, N.M., *Genesis* (The JPS Torah Commentary; Philadelphia: Jewish Publication Society, 1989).

—*Exodus* (The JPS Torah Commentary; Philadelphia: Jewish Publication Society, 1991).

Schneidau, H.N., *Sacred Discontent: The Bible and Western Tradition* (Baton Rouge, LA: Louisiana State University Press, 1976).

Searle, J.R., *Speech Acts; An Essay in the Philosophy of Language* (Cambridge: Cambridge University Press, 1969).

Seeligman, J.L., 'Aetiological Elements in Biblical Historiography', *Zion* 26.3-4 (1961): 141-69 (Hebrew).

Smith, S.H., '"Heel" and "Thigh"': The Concept of Sexuality in the Jacob-Esau Narratives', *VT* 40.4 (1990): 464-73.

Speiser, E.A., *Genesis* (AB; Garden City, NY: Doubleday, 1964).

Sternberg, M., *The Poetics of Biblical Narrative: Ideological Literature and the Drama of Reading* (Bloomington, IN: Indiana University Press, 1987).

Stevens, W., *The Palm at the End of the Mind: Selected Poems* (ed. H. Stevens; New York: Vintage Books, 1972 [1967]).

Tanakh: A New Translation of the Holy Scriptures according to the Traditional Hebrew Text (Philadelphia: Jewish Publication Society, 1985).

Todorov, T., *Mikhail Bakhtin: The Dialogical Principle* (trans. W. Godzich; Minneapolis, MN: University of Minnesota Press, 1984).

Trible, P., *God and the Rhetoric of Sexuality* (Philadelphia: Fortress Press, 1978).

Widengren, G., 'Myth and History in Israelite-Jewish Thought', in S. Diamond (ed.), *Culture and History: Essays in Honor of Paul Radin* (New York: Columbia University Press for Brandeis University, 1960): 467-95.

Yerushalmi, Y.H., *Zakhor: Jewish History and Jewish Memory* (Seattle: University of Washington Press, 1982).

INDEXES

INDEX OF REFERENCES

OLD TESTAMENT

INDEX OF AUTHORS

JOURNAL FOR THE STUDY OF THE OLD TESTAMENT

Supplement Series